SPY FOR FIDEL

Orlando Castro Hidalgo

SPY FOR FIDEL

E. A. Seemann Publishing, Inc.
Miami, Florida

To All Who Play the Great Game

"There are no leaders to lead us to honor, and yet
                without leaders we sally,
Each man reporting for duty alone, out of sight, out of
reach, of his fellow.
                . . . . .
"Not where the squadrons mass,
        Not where the bayonets shine,
Not where the big shells shout as they pass
        Over the firing-line;
Not where the wounded are,
        Not where the nations die,
Killed in the cleanly game of war—
        That is no place for a spy!
                . . . . .
"Trained to another use,
        We march with colours furled. . . . "

From "The Spies March" by Rudyard Kipling

Contents

Prologue

HALCYON DAYS, HAPPY DAYS, DAYS ALWAYS TO BE remembered. Endless miles of cane golden in the sun, the waters, cool and clear, of the tree-shaded Chorrillo River, the childhood friendships that would last a lifetime—these were preserved in that corner of the heart where political affairs do not intrude.

I, Orlando Castro Hidalgo, a young *campesino* from La Pedrera, near Puerto Padre, Oriente Province, Cuba, would see many things and have many adventures once I left this tiny spot which appears on no map, but La Pedrera would remain ever a part of me. Twists of fate would one day enable me to travel to the wonders of the world, and I would gaze upon the Eiffel Tower, the Nile and the Pyramids, Mont Blanc in Switzerland, ancient Athens, and the majestic structures of the city of Washington. Always, however, there was La Pedrera in the background, well and fondly remembered. And when there came those days that a big decision had to be made, it was the basic, earthy human being that made that decision, not the political creature which a Communist state had sought to contrive.

The youths of La Pedrera played baseball, the girls as well as the boys, for this was and has remained Cuba's favorite sport, verging on a national addiction. It was great fun to play, and wonderful fun also to watch local teams compete at the town stadium. I made pitcher on a juvenile team, and when the team won, I was always the hero, for I was the only pitcher. There wasn't much available in the way of transportation, and when travel to a nearby town was necessary, the team simply got on horses and rode there, sometimes arriving too worn out to play up to their usual standards.

From juvenile I graduated to the "amateur" team. As a substitute player I had the responsibility, in addition to playing, of also tending a stand which dispensed soft drinks, beer, and Bacardi rum. Raffles were held among the spectators—the prizes were bottles of Bacardi— but somehow no one ever won and the rum was then enjoyed by the players.

There were dances at the Salón de Cesáreo. The young men deposited nickels in the juke box and selected their partners. On one occasion I approached my friend Norma, took her hand, and asked her to dance. She pulled back her hand and reprimanded me, "You don't have to take my hand in order to dance with me." I desisted and replied that without holding her hand I could not dance with her. I could be independent: there were other willing girls about. It may be noted, however, that the small contretemps did not prevent me from marrying Norma years later.

One year I was selected as the best student at the rural school I was attending. This won me a trip to the capital city of Havana at the expense of the government. That was the first time I had ever been to Havana. Together with other prize students from around the country, I was taken on extensive sightseeing tours. The climax of the trip was a grand dinner hosted by President Fulgencio Batista and his wife, Marta. The day would come when I would be deeply involved in the struggle against Batista.

In the summertime of Cuba, the sun is bright, the skies are light blue and cloudless, and then a few clouds appear, and more, and by two in the afternoon the earth is being drenched in a torrential thunderstorm. The early fifties were the summer of the century; the first clouds had appeared, and they multiplied when Batista returned to power through a coup one cold night in March of 1952. He seized the government by force and he had to rule by force, and force engenders force.

I.

Revolution

THE FIRST ARMED ASSAULT AGAINST THE BATISTA establishment consisted of an attack against Moncada Barracks in Santiago de Cuba in 1953 by a group of young men. The revolutionary chief was a former student leader named Fidel Castro Ruz. When news of Moncada reached La Pedrera, two of the local men announced that they were off to join the rebels. I had no interest in politics at this time, but I did feel that this was quite heroic. Two days later, however, the heroes were located on a sugar-loading wharf. Their weapons were not rifles but bottles of Bacardi, and they remembered absolutely nothing about any intention of joining the rebellion. Such was revolution in La Pedrera in 1953.

By 1956 Fidel Castro had been tried, imprisoned, amnestied, and gone off to Mexico, from whence he returned to Oriente once again at the head of an armed expedition. A major uprising took place in Santiago, and now there were truly revolutionary stirrings in the land. Castro captured the imagination of much of the country's youth, and in La Pedrera clandestine rebel cells were organized. Initially these acted *por la libre,* but then they tied in with the growing national resistance movement.

I was caught up in the revolutionary fervor, and I joined one of the clandestine cells, unknown even to my family. So secret were such matters that only later did I learn that an uncle of mine was also an active rebel—neither of us was aware of the other's activities.

The authorities discovered that one Raimundo Castro—Castro is a common name in Oriente—was a member of the 26 of July rebel movement, and he fled into the hills. His home was burned to the ground by the Army, and a substantial number of troops were seen in the area. I was in bed with the mumps, but I arose and went out in an effort to ascertain what was going on. If the soldiers were hunting Raimundo Castro, perhaps he could be warned. My efforts were to no avail. Rifle fire was heard in the distance, and soon afterwards it was learned that Raimundo Castro had been killed. The official account given later was that he had been caught while attempting to set fire to a canefield in an act of sabotage. The local citizenry knew there had been heavy rains that night, however, and it would have been difficult for a person out in the open to light a match, let alone ignite an entire canefield.

Acts of sabotage, distribution of propaganda, procurement of weapons to be sent to rebel guerrillas, these were the functions of the clandestine movement in La Pedrera. On one occasion the underground learned that a sizable cache of weapons was stored in a private home some distance away. Four other rebels and I "borrowed" a Jeep and drove to the house at night. We disarmed a guard and, at pistol-point, got him to tell where the weapons were kept. We happily made off with the revolvers, rifles, shotguns, and ammunition that we found.

My first taste of combat came in an unexpected—and definitely frightening—manner. I had escorted another member of the underground, who was sought by the authorities, to a guerrilla encampment in the hills. While sleeping in the camp the night of my arrival, I was rudely awakened by an excited rebel who informed me that Rural Guards were approaching. Hearing the sound of nearby shooting, I jumped out of my hammock and raced from the hut in which I had been sleeping. Soldiers appeared to have the camp virtually surrounded, and the rebels, close to panic, were seeking a means to escape. The soldiers fired into the camp; we shot back into the foliage. Bullets whistled through the air, and I could see them perforating the trunks of palm trees.

4

The rebels scattered. Running in a crouch, sheltering myself as best I could, firing my few bullets as I ran, I managed to escape through a ravine. At one point a machine gun volley came so close that I had to fling myself flat on the ground. Examining myself for possible damage, I found that a bullet had pierced a pocket of my shirt, but had not touched me. In that pocket I carried a picture of the Virgin of Charity. I took it out—it had been creased by the bullet—and kissed it with gratitude.

I returned home safely. The day came, however, as it did to a good many young Cubans in those days, when I decided it was time to join the guerrillas in the Sierra Maestra Mountains. The exploits of the guerrillas were being reported by a rebel radio transmitter and recounted person to person throughout the province. Unable to quell the spreading rebellion, the governmental authorities resorted in desperation to increasingly ruthless repressive measures, especially in the cities and towns where the clandestine movement operated. It was highly dangerous for members of the underground to continue their work.

Six other youths from the area and I set out for the Sierra Maestra, aided on the way by persons sympathetic to the rebel cause. The main underground route to the guerrillas lay through the town of Bayamo, but we were warned by a clandestine contact that there were large numbers of troops in the area, and the authorities had rounded up the persons who had been helping recruits to reach the guerrillas.

We reversed our route and headed toward the north central portion of the province, where there were other guerrillas. After a considerable amount of walking, the group—now reduced to five members—made contact with and joined a rebel band operating near the Chaparra sugar mill, not far from the city of Puerto Padre. We had just about returned to our starting point.

The first days at the guerrilla base were spent in routine guard duty. Then, one rainy afternoon, word was received that an Army detachment was moving toward the camp, and we took up defensive positions. The Army attacked and we were soon forced to pull out, abandoning the camp. One of us was killed: a 14-year-old boy who came from a peasant family a few miles away. We recovered the body and returned it to the sorrowing family. No casket was available, so the body was wrapped in palm fronds and buried in the yard of the family's house.

5

After a while, in our freewheeling, characteristic style, our group left the band we had been with and joined another in the Sierra de Gibara. The main rebel units were designated as "columns," and ours was Column 14, commanded by Major Eddy Suñol. My first task was to help guard a number of Army men that had been captured, and in the following weeks we participated in several small ambushes and skirmishes. In the main, however, the government's military forces had withdrawn into their *cuarteles* and rarely ventured outside. The Army by now was largely demoralized, and we were becoming ever bolder, spreading our activities over widening areas.

Column 14 set forth to attack the Army post in the town of Velasco, but we found that the troops had hurriedly abandoned it upon learning of our approach. The citizens of the town joyfully greeted us and provided us with shoes, clothes, medicines, hammocks, and other supplies. I obtained a nylon sheet, truly a luxury because of its usefulness in covering oneself in a hammock during a rainstorm.

A siege of malaria and grippe struck the guerrillas, and I was among those who fell seriously ill. I was sent to the home of an aunt, and then my own home, where I was reunited with relatives and friends for the first time since I had embarked on my military career.

Once recovered, I joined the rebel unit I had been with that night of the ambush and my narrow escape, when I had taken a member of the underground into the hills. This unit was now a part of Column 12, commanded by Major Delio Gomez Ochoa. By this time—December of 1958—the civil war had reached its climax, the government position was rapidly deteriorating, and we rebels were clearly on the offensive.

The commanders of Columns 12 and 14 prepared an attack on the military, naval, and police installations in the city of Puerto Padre. The actual attack would be made by Column 12, while Column 14 would lay in ambush to trap any Army unit that might try to come to Puerto Padre from the *cuartel* at nearby Delicias. At midnight of December 24 the attack was launched. I participated in the assault against the Navy *cuartel,* a concrete building by the sea. The rebels held positions atop nearby houses and maintained an almost continuous stream of fire against the sailors. They returned the fire, refusing demands that they surrender. Throughout the night rifle fire and Molotov cocktails lit the night with their fury.

6

The rebel assault took its toll of the defenders, and by morning their gunfire was noticeably reduced. Then, when we thought they were about to make a substantial capture of weapons and prisoners, we saw that the sailors were dumping their guns and ammunition into the sea and jumping in after them, to make their escape by swimming away. The naval commander, meanwhile, maintained his own fire in order to cover the flight of his men, after which he surrendered and the post fell.

The Army post and police station also surrendered, and the city was firmly under our control. People flocked into the streets to see the *barbudo* liberators and invited us into their homes to be feted. The joy turned to fear, however, when it was rumored that the city was about to be bombed by the government's air force, and an exodus began from the city. Two fighter planes appeared overhead, circled and dived, but limited themselves to strafing runs outside the city at points where they believed there were rebel forces. Clearly the pilots did not want to inflict casualties on the civilian population.

A few days later the war came to an end. The nation floated on a euphoric cloud. Most of the population had been involved, in varying degrees, in the struggle to unseat the dictator, and now the national aurora had finally arrived. A far worse nightmare was approaching, but few saw it in those days of joy and victory and what was thought to be the restoration of democracy.

My military career did not end with the coming of peace. My unit was moved several times to different military posts, and the men were given formal military instruction. I was selected to become a recruit in a new marine corps that was being organized. Creation of the corps was the idea of Raúl Castro, who at this time was not yet adverse to following American models. The corps was established at Granma Base in Pinar del Río, but facilities were so primitive that they were virtually nonexistent and the recruits had to build them, in addition to their training.

The marine corps did not last long. Perhaps the Castro brothers feared that an elite military unit was a potential threat to their regime. Perhaps the rebel army resented establishment of a special military unit for which it saw no need. At any rate, one day the base commander summoned the marines and told us that the corps was too costly and that there were other forces, such as the police, that were in need of manpower.

The marine corps was dissolved and we were sent to Havana to become part of the Revolutionary National Police. I was assigned to the Sixth Precinct, where I did routine work: walk a beat, handle the front desk, operate the switchboard. I managed to get out of these tasks by joining the police baseball team, on which I was a pitcher.

A police combat battalion was organized, and I was picked to be a member. The regime was now confronted with the same problem that had vexed Batista: anti-Castro guerrillas were operating in the Escambray Mountains in south central Cuba, not far from a place that would come to be known as the Bay of Pigs. The police battalion was dispatched to the Escambray, where it spent weeks combing caves and canefields, flat lands and mountainsides looking for guerrillas. Only a few were captured. The police also spent a month cutting cane: most of the regular cutters had joined the rebels.

The police especially sought to capture a rebel leader known as "Captain Campito." Campito had fought against Batista, but later had turned against Castro, also. Campito knew the area in which he was operating so well that his pursuers never seemed able to come close to him. I began to suspect that he was a myth, but then local peasants would talk about him, and it was evident that Campito was very real, indeed. Our police unit never did succeed in capturing him.

In Central America, at this time, Cuban exiles were in training for an attack on Cuba, and in Cuba rumors circulated that the attack was imminent. The police battalion was transferred to Matanzas Province, where it was assigned the task of guarding a beach considered to be a possible landing point for invaders. The invasion did not materialize, and so the police made additional moves, finally being sent to a camp at a place called El Esperón in Pinar del Río Province, where the men were to receive more military training.

My combat days were not yet over.

II.

Invasion

A GREAT DEAL HAS BEEN SAID AND WRITTEN ABOUT the ill-fated Bay of Pigs invasion of April 1961. The planning and preparation, the last-minute crippling of the attack by the cancellation of further air raids on airfields, the lack of sufficient logistical support and air cover over the beachhead—all these are now history. The politicians have told their stories, the invaders have told theirs, but not much has ever been said by the foot sloggers on the government side who fought the invaders toe to toe. I was one of those infantrymen.

Early in 1961 it was public knowledge that Cuban exiles were building a military force in Central America. Whether these would be infiltrated into Cuba to carry out guerrilla operations, or whether a full-blown invasion was planned, was not clear. Cuba prepared for an attack. Completing its work in the Escambray Mountains, the police company to which I was attached was moved to Ganuza Beach in Matanzas Province to await a possible invasion. After several weeks, the unit was again transferred, this time to a camp known as El Esperón, near Caimito de Guayabal in Pinar del Río Province.

Early in the morning of April 15 air raids were carried out on several Cuban airfields. At El Esperón the *alarma de combate* was given, and we were told that the raids undoubtedly were the prelude to an invasion. The following day warships were seen off the coast of Pinar del Río (actually, this was a feint by the U.S. Navy to distract attention from the main landing point on the south coast of Matanzas).

On the morning of April 17, Monday, the camp loudspeakers sounded reveille at Esperón and we were quickly summoned into formation. We were told that enemy forces had carried out landings, and we must be prepared for battle. All leaves had been canceled following the Saturday air raids, and this cancellation remained in effect. Rumors flashed through the camp: a tremendous attack was coming, the Americans were going to land, heavy air raids were in prospect.

That afternoon the entire Police Combat Battalion was ordered to march to the nearby coast. (The battalion consisted of five companies of about ninety men each. I belonged to the Fifth Platoon of the Fourth Company. I led a seven-man squad.) We were set to work digging trenches. Five feet deep and zigzag in design, the trenches extended (although not continuously) for dozens of miles along the coast and the base of hills close by. Army and militia units also participated in the task. The trench-digging continued through most of the night, but the enemy did not appear.

When the digging was completed, we camouflaged the trenches with leaves and branches. We slept in the trenches as best we could—a sleep occasionally interrupted by false combat alarms sounded by sergeants who wanted to test their men.

At noon of April 18 we were called into formation and were informed we would be transported to the theater of operations, where the enemy had landed. Late that afternoon huge trucks arrived at the camp, and we climbed aboard. The ride lasted about four hours. We knew the general area in which we were heading, although not the precise point. We wondered and worried about what lay ahead for us, and thought of our families and sweethearts. Some took photographs of loved ones from their wallets and stared at them. Regrets were voiced, and there were complaints and occasional jokes, and some singing, too.

I was in an open truck and was able to recognize areas I knew, as we drove through. Then, as we approached the south coast, we began passing ambulances and small trucks converted to ambulances.

10

From our trucks we could see that these vehicles were carrying wounded militiamen and soldiers of the regular Army, but we saw no one in any other uniform, no members of the invading force. This impressed us; we realized the significance of what we saw: the invaders must indeed be fighting hard in order to be causing these casualties.

The trucks slowed to a stop by the road, and we jumped out. Sporadic firing could be heard in the distance. An airplane was heard overhead, and antiaircraft guns opened fire. The tracer bullets streaming through the dark sky were our first sight of combat.

We were warned to be on the alert for mines reportedly placed in the ground. The men gathered to get into formation, and as I stepped through sand, I felt a solid object under one of my booted feet. The foot suddenly developed a mind of its own; it refused to move further. I leaned over slowly and began to brush the sand away from my foot. Men near me noticed what was happening, and they stiffened, staring. My fingers felt hard, smooth matter. My heart beat rapidly, and I was close to panic. I gingerly continued brushing away the sand, and to my vast relief I was able to discern that what I was stepping on was only a large conch shell. The breath I exhaled was equaled by those of the men standing nearby.

The place at which we had arrived was near Larga Beach, although we could not see the ocean from where we were. This was a sandy area, spotted with rocks, clumps of shrubs, and mangrove trees. Burnt shrubbery and overturned buses gave evidence of recent combat. The buses had been transporting militia from the city of Cienfuegos and had been spotted and attacked by the invaders' aircraft.

We were told to make ourselves as comfortable as possible while awaiting further orders. We sprawled along the side of the road, our eyes warily searching the ground for signs of mines. Several men used their knapsacks as makeshift pillows.

We wore olive-green fatigues and kepis of the same color. We were equipped with Belgian rifles and Czech submachine guns, more than 200 rounds of ammunition each, and Soviet-made shovels and pickaxes. These were found to break easily, and most were discarded.

We remained in the area the rest of the night and until seven-thirty in the morning. Reports that were received indicated that there had been heavy fighting and that the invaders were in possession of some territory. We heard that the main damage to the invaders had been inflicted by government planes attacking the landing ships. We got little sleep that night. We listened to occasional firing in the distance, and talked among ourselves, knowing we would soon be in combat.

In the morning we were told we would march toward the enemy positions at Girón. Two lines were formed, on either side of the road, with about six feet between each man. We watched the skies: earlier a B-26 had skimmed in low, firing its machine guns, but had been driven off by antiaircraft fire. I had thought bullets were striking near me, but found that these were only the expended shells of the AA guns.

In titular command of the police battalion was the chief of police, Major Efigenio Ameijeiras, who arrived that morning. In actual command was Major Samuel Rodiles, a veteran of the 1956-1958 guerrilla war. Ameijeiras said he would lead his men into combat. Later, however, when contact with the enemy was established and firing began, he was seen heading toward the rear. We heard that he had been summoned by Fidel Castro.

The precise location of the invaders was unknown, and we therefore did not know just when we would go into battle. At nine o'clock in the morning we scrambled off the road when a B-26 came in on a strafing run. Two men in my company were hit.

That morning, before we had set out on our march, an Army officer had warned Ameijeiras not to try to advance. The officer reported that the invaders were fighting well, that probably they were made up of veterans of Korea and World War II, and that they had inflicted heavy casualties on the government forces, suffering few themselves. Whenever the government troops attempted to advance, he said, they were thrown back. Despite this news and advice, Ameijeiras declared that we would move forward, even if this were to be a suicidal advance.

As we marched ahead, it appeared that we might very well be involved in a suicidal attack. We passed militiamen seated by the side of the road, who, although they did not seem to be retreating, were not moving forward either. We noted considerable numbers of casualties not yet picked up by the ambulances. Questioned as to what the general situation was, the militia replied: "Every time we have gone into battle, we have been repulsed. Many of our men have been

12

killed." Asked to join our advance, the militia answered that they were awaiting their superiors, but these were nowhere to be seen.

We found one militia leader, but he refused to advance. He was promptly relieved of his command. The second-in-command of our police battalion, Captain Ricardo Carbó, took charge of the militia unit and got the men to move forward with us.

The road led over the beach, the ocean to the right of the men and swampland to their left. At around ten in the morning we received the first indications that we were entering combat: mortar shells fell into the ocean offshore, sending up great geysers of spray. Someone said that this was the Army carrying out target practice, and with this explanation we continued marching ahead. (Actually, these were shells from the invaders. Captured later on, their mortar men mentioned that they had been disconcerted when, upon dropping their shells near the advancing lines, they had seen the police unconcernedly continue to move forward.)

We came under enemy infantry fire, and our advance was now slow and exceedingly dangerous. I moved forward as best I could, at times running in a low crouch, sometimes slithering ahead on my stomach, going from shelter to shelter, a rock here, a hole in the sand there. The enemy mortar fire improved its aim, and the police casualties mounted. A member of my squad stood up to run forward, and at that precise moment was killed by the nearby explosion of a mortar shell. And then another man in the squad was killed. The company as a whole suffered some ten dead and a considerable number of wounded.

The invaders were fighting well. Nevertheless, we were able to advance. We pushed beyond Larga Beach, the enemy pulling back slowly, while maintaining heavy fire on the government forces.

At one point around noon, we were pinned down by concentrated fire from enemy machine gun nests. The advance appeared to be halted. It was then that six Soviet-built tanks arrived on the scene, much to our relief. The tanks blasted their way through the enemy strong points, forcing the invaders back again. We charged, following the tanks. The fast-moving tanks pulled ahead of us.

Soon after, however, we saw tanks coming back down the road. At first we thought these were enemy vehicles, but then recognized them as the same tanks that had been leading the advance. One of our officers waved down a tank and demanded to know why the tanks were pulling back. A soldier in the tank replied that they were having difficulty with their oil. The officer angrily asked: "How come it works to retreat? Why doesn't it work to advance? "

The tank men ignored the officer's remonstrations, saying they did not have to account to him. They closed the tank hatch. The infuriated officer tried to put his rifle into a slit in the tank with the evident intention of shooting its crew. Other men seized the officer and took away his weapon.

The tank rapidly proceeded back to the rear, as did three others. Their haste was so great that they ran over and killed a wounded man lying in their path. Other soldiers had to jump out of their way in order to avoid being crushed.

The tanks were retreating because two of their number had been destroyed by an enemy Sherman tank emplaced at a curve in the road. The Soviet-made tanks were especially vulnerable due to the fact that they carried, attached to their sides, fuel tanks which burst into flames when hit by gunfire.

There had been other instances of cowardice during the advance. At one point, an order was passed through the ranks to a certain unit telling it to move to the vanguard position. When the order reached that unit, most of the men denied belonging to it. On another occasion, a police captain hiding in a hole ordered his men to move forward, but refrained from doing so himself. A sergeant came over and wrathfully berated the officer, and followed this by socking him in the face.

The enemy tank that had forced the government tank column to retreat had situated itself among dense vegetation in a ravine, protected by rocks. The curve near which the tank was emplaced became known as the "Death Curve" because of the heavy fighting at this spot. A bazooka unit circled through the swamps on the left with the intention of striking the tank, but ran into enemy machine gun nests and had to pull back. Upon returning to the government lines, the unit's members were mistaken for enemy troops, and we opened fire on them. After a great deal of frantic yelling, the men managed to identify themselves and the firing ceased.

The Sherman was finally put out of action when a lieutenant fired a bazooka shot which scored a direct hit on it. The advance was able to continue, and we approached the town of Girón itself. (It is by the name of this town, rather than by the Bay of Pigs, that the invasion is officially known in Cuba.)

14

At three in the afternoon a heavy mortar attack rained down on us. There was another damaged and abandoned Sherman tank to one side of the road, and I headed toward it to find shelter from the close and continuous hail of shells.

A loud explosion close by—I felt and heard it, but saw nothing. I was being wafted through the air. There was no pain—I did not really know what was happening to me—perhaps I was dying . . . then after a second or two I lost consciousness.

I awoke slowly. My memory returned and I recalled the explosion. I was lying on a floor somewhere. It seemed to be nighttime, and I wondered whether I was a prisoner. My head throbbed with pain; it felt as if the whole thing were inflamed. I found that there was blood in my nose and mouth, and that I had received no medical treatment. I touched the blood, tasted it, thought bleakly, "I've been destroyed." I was terrified that I had lost my sight. I realized there were other human beings about, and I touched one nearby and felt cold flesh. The man was probably dead.

I learned later that my eyesight had been temporarily impaired and that I had received a wound on my forehead.

I heard a voice that I recognized. It was that of Juan de Dios, a member of my company who had been wounded earlier. I called out to him, startling him, because he thought all those around him were dead. De Dios came over and told me that we were in an improvised hospital in Jagüey Grande. He was able to get two attendants to place me on a stretcher and bandage me. Then I was taken to a hospital in another city. Here I was X-rayed and given necessary treatment. After a week, I was transferred to the Police Hospital in Havana, where I remained an additional three weeks.

In the meantime, the invasion had been repelled and destroyed, and Fidel Castro was in firm control of Cuba.

Training

BACK ON ACTIVE DUTY WITH THE POLICE, AFTER MY hospital stay and then a month's leave, I was stationed at the Fourth Precinct. Here I was assigned to the *Dirección General de Orden Publico*, an organization with wide responsibilities related to the maintenance of public order. My task was to check the passports and documents of persons preparing to leave the country.

I was with the D.G.O.P. for about half a year, and then the organization was transferred to the Ministry of the Interior. I went with it, and now was no longer with the police. I continued to do the same work as previously, until transferred to the ministry's Social Study and Prevention Department, which dealt with such matters as prostitution, drug addiction, and juvenile delinquency. The section not only tried to help prostitutes find legitimate work and steer potential delinquents away from trouble, it also kept an eye on clergymen and churchgoers, who, under the Communist system, were also considered to be potential troublemakers.

I used my time in Havana to good avail. I had discontinued my formal education upon completion of the sixth grade, but while in the marines had resumed studying and continued this during my police and ministerial employment. As a former member of the rebel army I was entitled to an education, and I took advantage of this opportunity to pursue my studies to the pre-university level.

Norma, my childhood friend from La Pedrera, was now teaching in Havana, and I began seeing her, and then courting her. We were married in July of 1965.

It was while I was at work at the ministry that my life took a drastic new turn.

When I was recruited by the *Dirección General de Inteligencia,* or D.G.I., I knew nothing about the organization, nor even that it existed. I was summoned by my chief at the Ministry of Interior and told: "I have been asked for a selection of the men under my command. You have been picked because you work well and have a good revolutionary background." I had not sought a transfer from my job, and now I was intrigued by what lay ahead, and a little concerned, too. I thought that perhaps I had been chosen by G-2, the widely feared secret police.

My recruitment was handled by a man I knew only as "Andres." Andres brought me lengthy forms to fill out, and asked many questions about my background. Andres never stated where all this was leading, but he did tell me: "Be prepared to leave. You will be taken to a certain place." The place was not identified, which did not add to my peace of mind. Then one day I was advised: "Tomorrow, instead of coming to work, be prepared for a trip. Bring a valise with clothes, and you will be picked up here at the ministry."

Two men came for me the next day in a Jeep: Andres and an individual who used the name "Victor." They drove me through the city and to an outlying area known as El Cano. Conversation during the trip was desultory; neither of the men was of a mind to tell me where we were going. Our destination turned out to be a cream-colored mansion, obviously once the property of a wealthy family. It had a pool, fine furniture, and tall palms on its extensive grounds. During the ride I was cautioned that I was to tell no one who I was, where I had come from, or what my background was. I was to use only my first name, and to ask none of the people I would meet about themselves. There were three or four other men in the house when I arrived, and in the next few days additional ones were brought in. I was assigned to a large, comfortable room. It had two beds and was equipped with television.

We were told that we were not permitted to leave the grounds,

17

nor to make any phone calls. We were not allowed to notify our families where we were. The only people we saw were Andres and Victor, and a caretaker who shunned conversation. I found myself filling out more forms, and answering more questions. Conversing among ourselves, we speculated as to why we were being kept in this house, how long we would be here, where we would be taken next. Some thought our stay in the house was some sort of psychological test, to see how well we could endure being cooped up for a length of time. We questioned each other to see if anyone knew more than the others, but no one seemed to have been told much.

Food was brought in from outside, and we were supplied with books and magazines. We occupied ourselves reading, swimming, playing chess and Ping-Pong, and talking about our strange situation. A wry comment was, "After this millionaire's vacation, what terrible thing is in store for us? "

The "vacation" lasted a week. One night we climbed aboard two Jeeps and were driven for an hour until we came to a place known as Loma de Tierra, about five miles outside Havana and near the road running between that city and Güines. The Jeeps turned onto a driveway partially lined with palm trees and pulled up in front of two red-roofed, light-colored buildings, one smaller than the other and probably once the servants' quarters. The buildings were set on a small farm, and numerous trees, closely spaced, obscured them from the road. I did not know it at the moment, but this was the training school for Cuba's intelligence service. Previously most Cuban agents had received their instruction behind the Iron Curtain; now they would be trained in Cuba.

There were already about twelve other students in the house, although our group did not see them until the following morning. The other men were sleeping in the smaller house; our group was assigned to a dormitory in the main building. We were provided with complete sets of olive-green military fatigues, plus army boots. We were also assigned numbers—mine was 28—which we were to use for identification purposes in lieu of names.

The students were summoned to hear a preliminary briefing in the school's auditorium by the director, a man about 40 years old who used the name "Marrero." He admonished us that we were not to reveal our names to other students, nor to question them. We were told that we were being prepared for service in D.G.I.—much to our surprise, for most thought they had been taken into G-2. Although the intelligence service was civilian, the training would be along military lines, for, "if the future Intelligence official is to be well-disciplined when he is abroad, he must receive military training, so that he will be a better-organized and better-disciplined person." Marrero wore a military uniform (but no rank insignia), and the instructors would include other military men.

The director told us that as yet a precise training program had not been worked out, nor was it certain who the instructors would be. The school was in the process of being organized. The director said: "The course will be a long one. We will try to make it a good one." In this talk, and in lectures by other officials in the following days, the students were informed what D.G.I. was, how it was organized, what its functions were.

Representatives of different sections of D.G.I. began coming to the school to instruct the students. One of these was "Fermín," whom I later came to know as head of D.G.I.'s Brazil desk. Fermín gave a general talk on the nature of intelligence work. Other officials lectured on recruitment, communications, photography, information-gathering, and diverse other matters and methods that concern an intelligence service. There was also a course on general culture, providing the rudiments of music and other arts, as well as the basics of world history.

A schedule of activities was worked out for the students. The timetable for getting up, for meals, for classes, for lights-out governed their daily life. Sports included volleyball, baseball, and Ping-Pong, and there was chess for those who wanted it. We were given some time off, usually on weekends. The system of numerical identifications was found to be impractical, especially outside the school. How were two students to greet each other if they met in, say, a restaurant? "Hello, 26." "Hello, 12." So a system of code names was adopted, and mine became "Osvaldo." This code name remained with me throughout my intelligence career, and it was the name I bestowed upon my second son.

In the photography course we learned the operation of different types of cameras. We were taught how to take ordinary photographs with 35-millimeter cameras, and how to photograph documents with the small Minox. We were instructed on taking photos from cars, photos of distant objects, photos of a moving person. Our preliminary work was in class, followed by photography practice under real conditions on city streets. We also learned the use of microdots and of latent photography for the secret transmittal of information. It was demonstrated that material can be photographed and reduced to a size little larger than a pinhead, and this microdot can then be concealed under a stamp or amidst writing in a letter. Through the use of latent photography, a print can be placed on a sheet of special paper, but remains invisible until properly developed. The paper may be in the form of a postcard, and the phony postcard can be sent through the mails to its destination, with its true contents not being apparent to the naked eye.

We received instruction in various methods that can be utilized to recruit persons, generally foreigners, who would be useful to Cuban Intelligence. We were told that our recruitment lessons were based on the experiences of Soviet Intelligence. Most emphasis was placed on recruitment based on ideological sympathies: a person who was in accord with the Cuban Revolution would likely be susceptible to overtures. Other recruitment methods that were described were blackmail—forcing a person to cooperate; sex—utilizing sex to entrap a person; and money—purchasing a person's services. We were also told about "recruitment under another flag." In this method, a person whose sympathies were with the "North Americans" would be approached by a Cuban agent posing as a C.I.A. agent, and asked to undertake a task. He would think he was doing this for the C.I.A., but actually it would be for D.G.I. The task assigned might be, for example, to have the person join an exile organization and report on its activities. He would believe his reports were for the benefit of Washington; instead they would be going to Havana. The least desirable form of recruitment was that carried out through the use of money. Persons whose services were purchased might well also sell their services to an enemy. We were told that a potential recruit should be studied carefully before an approach was made: the future agent's habits, friends, likes and dislikes—all this should be scrutinized, because any of these factors might later have a bearing on the person's work for Cuban Intelligence.

Communications are of vital importance to espionage agents, and we learned of a wide range of communications methods. Whatever the method used, we were advised that all intelligence messages were to be transmitted in code. We were shown how messages could be

20

converted into five-digit sets of numbers, a basic type of code. Messages transmitted in ordinary letters, we were told, could be written in invisible ink, to be developed by the person receiving the letters. An agent might find a radio to be useful, but he might also find himself using such simple things as thumbtacks. If agent A was to meet agent B, and agent A knew he was being followed and wanted to warn B, he could leave a yellow thumbtack in a post or a tree at a prearranged place. A red tack would mean severe danger; a white tack meant that everything was normal. Spy rings had in the past been broken up, the instructors warned, because of breaches in communications, sometimes among the agents themselves, sometimes in communications with their headquarters in their homelands.

The use of tacks or nails stuck in wood were a form of signal, but we were also told of another kind of signal. This was a danger signal, and we were to be on the watch for it among subagents or other persons with whom they might be working. A strange phone call, a puzzling telegram, these might indicate the person was in contact with the enemy. The person might receive a letter from abroad in which a "sick uncle" was mentioned, an uncle who was desirous of seeing him—this could be a secret message ordering an enemy agent to report to his home country.

Although there was talk in the classes of sophisticated communications equipment, we did not see any of it. Some instructors were openly resentful of the Russians over this. Having worked in Intelligence they knew that the Russians had good equipment, but were not supplying it to the Cubans. We were told we would have to make do with the inferior equipment that was available to us.

In preparation for serving abroad, we learned of two areas with which we must become familiar regarding the place (presumably a city) in which we would work: "operational situation" and "operational resources." The "operational situation" consisted of the characteristics of the city and its population as a whole. The intelligence agent must know the city's communications, transportation systems, economic life, politics, streets, and social composition. "Operational resources" referred, simply, to places and persons that could be helpful in transmitting messages. A hole in a tree or a wall could be used for depositing a message, to be picked up later by another person: this would be an operational resource. So would a place of contact—a café, a park, a path by a river—where two agents could meet. An inanimate object in which a message could be concealed was a "dead mailbox"; a "live mailbox" was a person who received messages in his home and then turned them over to another agent. Also considered to be resources were "places for passing," that is, locations where messages or objects could quickly be given by one person to another, without onlookers being likely to notice anything. Subways were considered best for this kind of transference.

"Sources of information" were another subject of study for us as future espionage agents. The foreign ministry of a country was cited as a prime source for useful information, as are most government departments. We were instructed on how to penetrate an organization in order to obtain information from it. The first step was to study in as great a detail as was feasible the personnel who worked in that organization. This would include gathering data on the type of people employed, where they lived, where they ate, their habits, vices, weaknesses, friends, how they were selected for their jobs. The next step was to pick an agent, or perhaps a willing third party, who appeared qualified to become friendly with one or more of the employees of the target organization. Then the process would begin of befriending an employee, and eventually extracting information from him. We student spies were told that when we used a subagent (often a local national) we must treat that person well, must keep him content, must see that his life was agreeable as possible. He must be complimented on tasks done well, but he must also be reprimanded when reproof was called for. The Cuban official must also "watch over" a subagent's political ideology.

These were the courses directly related to intelligence work. Other courses rounded out our general preparation for governmental service, especially duty abroad. There were political classes which dealt with politics both at home and abroad, practical as well as theoretical. We would break up into small groups of four or five men each and study and discuss Fidel Castro's latest speech. Instructors would lecture on Cuba's international policies, especially in relation to those of other countries, "socialist" as well as "imperialist." We also learned about such matters as philosophy, political economy, historic materialism, and dialectic materialism.

There was instruction on how an Intelligence official was to behave abroad. We were told we would have a *trabajo de manto* (a cover job) which would conceal our work as espionage agents. This cover would probably consist of a regular post on the diplomatic staff of the Cuban embassy to which we were assigned. We were told that the more careful and conscientious we were about our cover jobs, the better we could carry out our intelligence tasks. It was made clear, however, that intelligence work always had priority over all other work. If we were in the midst of a diplomatic task, and an intelligence job had to be done, the diplomatic work had to be postponed. As part of our cover, we were told we would involve ourselves in the normal activities of diplomatic life: go to cocktail parties, attend cultural acts, be present at official functions, and in general live exactly as regular diplomats did. Correct behavior at all times was stressed. Also emphasized was the necessity of maintaining security. Important papers were to be kept locked up, and Intelligence personnel were never to discuss their work with outsiders or in places where they might be overheard, or where there might be listening devices. We were cautioned that such devices might be planted in our homes, even our bedrooms, by the counterintelligence organizations of the countries in which we were stationed. Particular care must be taken, we were told, to protect the identities of other agents, as well as the agents' addresses.

We lived under strict military discipline. We wore our olive-green fatigues at all times, and we had to assemble in formation for roll call in the morning, at the raising and lowering of the flag, before meals, before classes, and before retiring at night. We were required to enter the dining room in silence, and there could be no rattling of cutlery against plates. We were instructed in the use of various types of weapons, among them Browning pistols, Belgian rifles, and Czech submachine guns. We were taught how to disassemble, assemble, and maintain these weapons, and then, on a target range, we learned how to fire them. Away from the school, we were told to identify ourselves as students at a military-political school. We were not to say we were in Intelligence, not even if we should happen to be arrested for anything, or even to our wives (an order which I chose to overlook). We were periodically taken to the Naval Hospital for physical examinations, and here we identified ourselves as being members of a "special unit" of the Ministry of Revolutionary Armed Forces.

Despite the gravity of its purpose, the intelligence school had some of the characteristics of male schools anywhere. There was a sports program (karate was obligatory). There was the school disci-

23

plinarian, an Army sergeant who demanded strict adherence to military norms—he insisted that before a pitcher of water could be moved from one dining room table to another, formal permission had to be asked of him. There was the school "mascot," student No. 11, who was liked by all but who never seemed to do anything right. There was the school prankster, No. 5, who during target practice would let out a yell and fall as if he had been accidentally shot—and then one day he was injured by a blank shell fired close by, and when he yelled no one believed him. I was not averse to pulling practical jokes of my own. On one occasion, during a class on weapons, I managed to slide a branch into the barrel of a fellow student's submachine gun, where it was found during inspection by the apoplectic sergeant.

The school had its equivalent of "the old boys." In this case these were a group of hard-core Communists who held their own meetings, from which the other students were barred. The Communists considered themselves to be superior because of their political education, and they claimed to be knowledgeable about almost everything, all of which engendered a good deal of resentment among the rest of us. We noticed, with ironic appreciation, that the Communists even preferred to fight among themselves.

The economy of Cuba is heavily dependent on the country's sugar and other crops, and therefore participation in harvesting is a civic duty expected of all citizens, those who live in cities as well as those in rural areas. We at the intelligence school were not exempted from this "voluntary" work. All had to put in time in the fields. We were told, "To be a good official you must also be a good worker."

Cuba has its own version of Stakhanovism, known as *emulación*. At the school, we were divided into *núcleos*. Weekly records were posted on a bulletin board so that the progress of each nucleus could be seen by all. On one occasion, because I had done very well in studies, discipline, sports, and "volunteer" work, I was honored as a "vanguard" worker.

All told, there were about thirty students at the school. Some arrived later than others; a number left earlier, apparently to fill D.G.I. personnel requirements. Only one student was expelled, and this was evidently due to something in his past, not because of any occurrence at the school.

The full course of studies was to have lasted one year. After eight

24

months, however, most of the individual courses had been just about completed, and the instructors were coming only sporadically. To help fill in the schedule, lessons in French and English were added to the studies.

One afternoon, some nine months after I had arrived at the school, I was summoned to the Director's office. This meant that either I was to be admonished about something or was to be released from further study. It turned out to be the latter. The director complimented me on my work and my behavior and informed me that my studies were complete. I was told to pack my personal possessions, and to set aside those things that belonged to the school. When I emerged from the office, other students gathered around to ask me why I had been summoned, and when I happily told them, they congratulated me warmly.

The next day I was taken from the school by an official of D.G.I.'s Section III.

IV

Intelligence

SECTION III WAS THE "ILLEGAL SECTION" OF D.G.I. ITS basic duty was to carry out espionage and counterespionage in the United States, Canada, and Mexico. A major function was spying on the C.I.A. and Cuban exile organizations engaged in anti-Castro activities. The offices of Section III were located in a gray, three-story house on Línea Street in the Vedado suburb of Havana. Nothing indicated the nature of the work conducted inside the building. In order to camouflage its activities, the section had a sign across the front of the building which proclaimed, *Prevención de Incendios* (Prevention of Fires). There was no fire-fighting equipment to be seen, however.

The subsection located in the upper portion of the building was in charge of operations at the Intelligence centers in Mexico, Canada, and the United Nations. It also handled the training of *oficiales* assigned to serve at these centers. The grounds and first floors were occupied by the *Buró C.I.A. y Contrarevolución.* Technically one bureau, in actuality there were two separate units, and eventually D.G.I. did split them into two distinct bureasu. The *Buró C.I.A. y Contrarevolución* was headed by "Demetrio," a onetime teacher, who had formerly worked in a section of G-2 which kept watch on the foreign embassies in Havana. Under him was "Menéndez," who also acted as chief of the counter-C.I.A. section. Another official, "Cándido," headed the *contrarevolución* section, which spied on the activities of Cuban exiles.

The work within the various sections often overlapped, and at times there was also involvement with G-2, whose task was to uncover and eliminate anti-regime activities inside Cuba. Liaison was maintained with G-2, and when G-2 caught someone who had been infiltrated into Cuba, or had knowledge of infiltrations, copies of the tapes and transcripts of the interrogations carried out by G-2 were turned over to D.G.I. If D.G.I. wanted particular information from a prisoner, a request was made to G-2, which would then try to elicit the data required. Of special interest were details about the operations of a vessel named the *Rex*, which was known to bring infiltrators to Cuba. Through information that had been gathered, D.G.I. had been able to build up a description of this vessel, which during the daytime appeared to be a commercial ship, but at night became a well-armed warship. Small, fast boats were believed used to carry infiltrators from the *Rex* to the Cuban shore.

D.G.I. also on occasion sought the cooperation of the *Comites de Defensa de la Revolución,* neighborhood vigilance committees which keep watch on the citizenry. If D.G.I. needed information about a certain person—perhaps someone who had lived in Cuba but was now involved in exile activities in the States—an *oficial* would question members of the C.D.R. in the place where that person had resided. A small problem was presented by the fact the D.G.I. was—and still is—virtually unknown in Cuba, and the security-conscious C.D.R. members cooperated only with G-2. C.D.R. offices had lists of G-2 agents to whom they were authorized to facilitate any requested information. When D.G.I. needed data, the tactic was adopted, therefore, of having an official go to the C.D.R., tell them he was new at G-2, and ask them to check with G-2 headquarters. G-2 would already have been advised by D.G.I. that one of its men was going to see the C.D.R., and so when the check was made, G-2 would vouch for the individual. The *comites* did not know that in reality they were dealing with the Intelligence service.

Upon leaving the D.G.I. school, I was assigned to work in the *contrarevolución* unit of Section III. My tasks amounted to counterespionage by remote control. The unit was concerned with infiltrating and spying on exile organizations operating out of Miami. I was given the *expedientes* (dossiers) of a number of key exile figures, and my task was to build up information about these persons with the view of finding a way to place a D.G.I. informer close to them. As a case officer, I had to delve into the background and relationships of not only the target individual, but also his relatives, friends, co-workers, and acquaintances. As this detailed information was gathered, I watched for possible opportunities which D.G.I. could exploit (a friend of the target individual known to be in need of funds and perhaps susceptible to bribery, a co-worker with a relative still in Cuba and therefore subject to coercion, and so on).

The most important of my *expedientes* was that of Eloy Gutiérrez Menoyo. Menoyo had been one of the leaders of a sizable guerrilla organization that had fought the Batista regime during the Revolution. Once the rebels had won, the organization was dissolved. Subsequently, Menoyo assisted in uncovering a major conspiracy aimed at toppling Castro, but later turned against Castro and fled to the United States. He helped set up an exile organization named Alpha 66, which became known for its raids against shipping off Cuba.

D.G.I. believed that Menoyo was in the process of bringing weapons to isolated spots on the Cuban coast and concealing them there, to be picked up and used at a future date. Reports received from Miami indicated that Menoyo himself planned to infiltrate into Cuba, and therefore D.G.I. and G-2 were conducting an investigation to ascertain which of Menoyo's friends in Cuba might be making preparations to assist his eventual arrival. It was felt that Menoyo would need the help of a "reception team" of local fishermen in order to be able to come ashore without being detected by the authorities, and likely fishermen were also being investigated.

I did not work in this section of D.G.I. long enough to see completion of the Menoyo *expediente*. Menoyo did infiltrate into Cuba in an effort to launch a new guerrilla campaign, and he was captured and imprisoned. By this time, however, I had been transferred to another department.

Another file which I handled was that of Andres Nazario Sargen, also a top figure in Alpha 66. The Sargen family was from Matanzas Province, and an investigation was under way to determine whether a connection could be found with any fishermen in that area. D.G.I.

and G-2 were seeking to ascertain who might be serving, or might in the future serve, on "reception teams" for Alpha infiltrators or for weapons that were being buried on cays and near beaches. The investigators were also trying to find out whether Sargen was in contact with any friends inside Cuba. The file was being built up, and eventually a plan would be prepared for consideration by the chief of D.G.I., Manuel Piñeiro. This plan would suggest methods by which it might be possible to penetrate Alpha, perhaps to place a spy or informer close to Sargen.

A third case on which I worked was that of a doctor, an orthopedist, who had participated in anti-Castro activities in Cuba and had been found out, but had managed to escape to the United States. In Miami the doctor was again active in the anti-Castro movement. As was the usual procedure, a detailed study was undertaken of relatives and friends of the doctor who were still in Cuba, and out of this study two possible approaches were being developed. A brother of the doctor was serving a prison term, and consideration was given to offering his release in return for cooperation by the doctor with D.G.I. If he would secretly supply Intelligence with information about exile activities, his brother would eventually be released—or so he would be told. The second approach would involve another relative who had applied for permission to leave Cuba. The permission would be granted—provided the man agreed to spy on the doctor for D.G.I. What if the man acceded and then reneged once he was in the States? This presented no problem: D.G.I. would simply keep his wife and children in Cuba as hostages. And if the man were to decide that, under the circumstances, he did not wish to go to the States, after all? That was no problem, either: he would be confronted with evidence that he had been involved in clandestine activities and told that he would be brought to trial unless he did cooperate. Thus does a police state "recruit" unwilling agents.

I handled four cases in the short time I served in Section III. The fourth file was that of Miguel Díaz Isalgué, a veritable Scarlet Pimpernel who was believed to have made numerous secret trips in and out of Cuba. Isalgué was well-experienced in this type of work: while in exile in Miami during the Batista dictatorship he had run weapons into Cuba for the Castro rebels. Later he had turned against Castro, as had Menoyo, and begun working against Castro's regime. Isalgué had succeeded in setting up a clandestine network in Cuba,

29

and had even recruited an Army *comandante* as a member. D.G.I. and G-2 knew that Isalgué had reception teams composed of fishermen in Matanzas Province, and possibly Las Villas Province also. An effort was under way to infiltrate agents into these teams.

It was learned that Isalgué had utilized his mother's home in Havana as a secret meeting place with his contacts in the area. The home was placed under close surveillance: all correspondence was opened and checked, the telephone was tapped, phone calls to and from the States were tape-recorded. Isalgué's friends were being investigated to see whether any were working with him. Despite the extensive effort made by the authorities, however, they did not succeed in capturing the elusive Isalgué.

In the course of gathering information for my various files, I had occasion to talk with a Cuban woman who had worked as a spy in Miami for the Cuban government. Marta A. González, a divorcée with a fair face and figure, in her thirties, had been trained by "Menéndez" in intelligence work and had been sent to the States. She had entered the country as a refugee in April of 1962. Becoming a part of the exile milieu, she presumably dispatched such information as she could gather about the activities of anti-Castro organizations. About a year and a half after her arrival, she returned to Cuba. There she published a book, *Bajo Palabra* (Under Oath), a caustic account of the life of Cuban exiles in the States. The book said nothing about the authoress being an Intelligence agent.

In her book, Marta González indicated that disillusionment with the United States was the cause of her return to Cuba. She told me a different story, however. She had been working under orders from Chafik Homero Saker Zenni, chief of the Intelligence Center within the Cuban delegation to the United Nations. Although travel of Cuban diplomats was restricted by the U.S. government to New York, Saker came to her one day and told her she had to leave, evidently because he suspected that the U.S. authorities were on to her activities and might be about to arrest her. He took her in his car and drove to Texas, where, posing as an American, she crossed into Mexico, from there to return to Cuba. (In her book, Mrs. González said that she went from the United States to Canada, and from there returned to Cuba.)

I was in Section III for three months. Subsequently I was transferred to the personnel selection department, where my work was not much different than it had been in the C.I.A. and counterrevolution bureau. My function was to put together reports of men who had been chosen as possible members of D.G.I. The selection was made by party and governmental organizations which had been requested to submit the names of their best men. All the information that could be obtained about these candidates was put together, and this was studied to see whether the men were suitable material for D.G.I. My job was to gather the various reports on each individual, and then to write an account summarizing what I had found regarding the individual's good and bad points. Final selection was made by the departmental chief.

I worked in the personnel section for only two and a half months. I was then transferred to Section II-2. My chief had asked me if I would like to change positions, and I had replied, yes, I would prefer to be engaged in intelligence work rather than the desk job I was now doing. Section II-2 had been set up as a result of the breaking of diplomatic relations with Cuba by all of the Latin American countries except Mexico. Cuba then established Intelligence centers in France, Spain, England, and Italy whose function was not only to handle espionage activities in Europe, but also to serve as a liaison between Havana and its agents in Latin America.

At Section II-2 I learned that I was to be sent to Paris, a fact which thoroughly delighted both my wife and me.

Headquarters for Section II-2 was located in what had once been the large, two-story home of a private family in the city of Marianao, adjoining Havana. The building was also where *oficiales* received their final training before being sent to European posts. By having headquarters and school in the same building, students were enabled to study the actual operations of the centers to which they were being assigned. Thus, I had access to messages sent to and from the Paris Center, and in this way became acquainted with the work carried out there.

Chief of Section II-2 at this time was Alberto Boza-Hidalgo Gato, an affable individual whom I had first met when Boza-Hidalgo had made occasional trips to the Intelligence school. Boza-Hidalgo's career in D.G.I. followed a rocky road. After I went abroad to serve in France, I heard that Boza-Hidalgo had suffered disciplinary action, evidently because of a lack of sufficient enthusiasm for his work, and perhaps also because he was not as ideologically militant as was

31

deemed desirable. Despite these failings, Boza-Hidalgo managed to reinstate himself in the good graces of his superiors and was sent to serve in the Intelligence Center within Cuba's United Nations delegation. There he became involved in espionage against the United States, and as a result, upon taking a trip to Cuba, he was barred by the U.S. government from reentering this country.

Part of the training I underwent in Section II-2 amounted to a refresher course on what I had learned at the Intelligence school. Studied again were such matters as how to arrange a clandestine meeting with another person, how to pass messages from one person to another, how to spot and evade anyone who might be following you. A large portion of my instruction, however, was directly related to the position and work I would assume in Paris. I was briefed on diplomatic rules, behavior, and protocol, and I delved into the French language, French politics, French economy, and information in general about Paris and the country. At night I attended classes on the arts at the National Council of Culture. Since I could not identify myself as being with the Intelligence service, my "cover" was that I belonged to the Foreign Commission of the Communist Party.

I was told that all friendships I might make in Paris had to be reported to the *jefe* of the *Centro*. In the Intelligence viewpoint, one did not have private friends abroad: acquaintanceships were supposed to have some bearing on the Intelligence work one was doing. Conversely, people who approached Intelligence personnel with a view to establishing a relationship were open to suspicion: they might be planted by the local counterintelligence service. The *jefe* had to be informed of any approach that was made, who had made it, how it was made, and the apparent intentions of the person involved.

The trainees were warned to beware constantly of counterintelligence services. We were told that every diplomat was an object of interest to counterintelligence, and for an Intelligence official everything outside of the *Centro* was a potential threat, a possible trap. We were especially warned about relationships with women, no matter how casual these associations might be, since the women might be working for counterintelligence.

Practical training at II-2 consisted mainly of planning and carrying out contact work on the streets of Havana. Two students would prepare a plan for meeting at a specified place at a certain hour.

They were supposed to do this without being seen by anyone who might be following either of them. To make this practice highly realistic, actual surveillance was carried out by agents of G-2. We would work up a contact plan and then submit it to our chief, who would usually inform G-2. G-2 was not always told, but we did not know when it was or wasn't. As part of the exercise, we were required to report later whether we had been under surveillance, and if so, to provide details about the men and the vehicles that had followed us. On one occasion a trainee reported that he had spotted five G-2 cars. Later, to his chagrin, he learned that that day G-2 had not followed him at all.

Ordinarily, an *oficial* had to undergo about one year's practical training before being sent abroad, but in my case this was cut to three months. The Paris *Centro* was shorthanded and in need of a new official. One phase of my training that was eliminated was a period of work at the Ministry of Foreign Relations, where I would have learned at firsthand the functioning of Cuban diplomacy. The purpose would have been to enable me to pose more knowledgeably as a diplomat while abroad.

Before leaving for Paris, I went before the Party Commission within D.G.I., composed of Communist Party members in D.G.I. All officials going abroad had to be investigated—"processed" was the preferred word—by the commission. Approval by this group amounted to granting membership in the Communist Party. It was felt that only persons acceptable for Party membership were fit to serve Cuba abroad. I was subjected to several days of interrogation. Questions ranged from my knowledge of Marxism and views on Viet Nam to my role in the Revolution and the political positions of my relatives and friends. I was asked about my wife's opinions regarding the Revolution. I was careful not to reveal that a few years earlier, before we were married, she had applied for permission to leave Cuba and go to the United States. Although this was an official record, apparently no one in D.G.I. had checked back and discovered this.

I won approval from the commission. Actually, this "processing" was little more than a formality, since the commission members knew that for a person to have come this far, he must already have been well-investigated and able to prove his worth. I was further aided by the presence on the commission of two men who had studied with me at Intelligence school.

Official papers from the Ministry of Foreign Relations, a last chat with the section chief, and a farewell dinner at the Mandarin Chinese Restaurant (which served Cuban food; Chinese food, like many other things, was lacking in Cuba), and I was ready to take up my post in Paris.

V.

Embassy

PARIS–CITY OF GAIETY AND COLOR, CITY OF ROMANCE, city of the world. We had thought a great deal about Paris in the past months; now our dreams were reality. We settled into our new apartment, went sightseeing, took long walks, and savored delightful foods and beautiful wines. Paris is a worthy goal for a diplomat from any nation, and for a young couple who had never traveled abroad to be given their first foreign post in Paris was wish fulfillment to the highest degree.

This trip was to be our second honeymoon. It would end in a nightmare.

I became acquainted with the staff of the Cuban Embassy and learned the operations of the Intelligence section and the diplomatic mission. Virtually the entire staff—except the ambassador and the counselor—were Intelligence personnel. They doubled as "diplomats." I was an *oficial* of D.G.I.; at the same time I held the post of *tercer secretario* and was the embassy's protocol officer. Paychecks were issued by the Ministry of Foreign Relations; I earned $600 per month, considerably more than the $200 the D.G.I. had been paying me in Havana.

The Cuban mission maintained its chancellery on the fourth floor of a building at 3 Rue Scribe. Here the routine matters of diplomacy were handled. The *oficiales* issued visas, dealt with trade matters, and assisted visitors not concerned with intelligence operations.

The ambassador, Baudilio Castellanos, had his residence in a building at 60 Avenue Foch, and this was officially known as the *Embajada de Cuba.* The Intelligence section maintained its offices here—an indication of the importance attached to this operation. The only other office, other than the ambassador's own, was the code room.

The building at 60 Avenue Foch was typical of those in this area near the Arch of Triumph. It was an edifice of unpainted blocks, maintained near-white through the assiduous use of sand and hot water. The avenue was wide and amply shaded by luxuriant trees; the grass was well tended. This was an aristocratic neighborhood, aristocratic in lineage as well as in appearance, for it had more than its share of princes, dukes, and counts living there. The Cuban Embassy enjoyed the comforts of high-ceilinged rooms and wide corridors.

The residence was reached by an elevator. On the third floor, two small vestibules led from the elevator to two apartments. The apartment on the left was occupied by private individuals. The one on the right bore a metal plaque which identified this as the *Embajada de Cuba.* Visitors rang a bell; this sounded in the kitchen, and someone would open the large, heavy, wooden front door. This door opened onto a corridor. To the left were the kitchen, the code room, the code official's quarters, and the bedrooms of the ambassador's children, as well as a conference room. To the right was a large ballroom where receptions and cocktail parties were held, then a small sitting room and the quarters of the ambassador and his wife.

Toward the middle of the apartment were the servants' quarters and the *Centro,* the Intelligence center. This occupied two rooms. One of these, equipped with desks and typewriters, was the office where paper work was done by the D.G.I. staff, the writing of reports and messages. On the walls were photographs of Ernesto "Che" Guevara and Camilo Cienfuegos, heroes of Cuba's Revolution. Fidel Castro has, in unusual modesty, never encouraged the display of his own picture, and there was none in this room. The second room, smaller than the office, contained photographic equipment and a large, old-fashioned safe, about four feet high. When necessary,

36

this room served as a darkroom for developing photographs. Within the safe each *oficial* kept a metal box containing copies of his reports, as well as any other documents or private papers that he wanted to store.

No guard was maintained at the Embassy because the code officer was always on duty, and usually servants and one or more members of the staff were also on the premises. On Sundays, when the code official took time off and left the Embassy, the Intelligence personnel rotated turns on duty.

For communications with Havana and with other Cuban diplomatic missions, the Embassy relied on various methods. The telephone could be used for nonconfidential messages. A Teletype was utilized for coded messages, especially to Havana and to the Cuban Embassy in London. Particularly sensitive messages were coded and dispatched by diplomatic couriers, who came to the Embassy every fifteen days. There were two codes: one utilized by the code officer, and one known only to and used by the Intelligence chief and his second in command. As an additional precaution, names and addresses in Intelligence reports were excised and dispatched separately.

The *jefe de la Inteligencia* in Paris was Armando López Orta, about 32 years old, a lawyer. López's revolutionary credentials consisted in having participated to a small extent in clandestine activities at the University of Havana. He had been at his post in Paris a year and a half when I arrived, and he would remain until three days after I left. His code name was "Arquimides." He was not a member of the Party, having been assigned to Paris before membership became a requirement for overseas duty. López was affable, liked a good joke, and treated his co-workers well. He worked hard himself, and he expected his staff to do likewise. His was a tight ship, but not an unhappy one.

Although he spent most of his time working, López was not resistant to the delights of Paris. He agilely managed to combine work and pleasure, undeterred by a pretty and charming wife, jealous though she was, and by two children. While carrying out routine tasks in his capacity as First Secretary, López often had occasion to converse with visitors to the chancellery. If the visitor was female, he would invariably speak with her, provided she was young and pretty, and as invariably would shunt her off to an aide if she were neither.

He always had time for the attractive, always had something "important" to do when the unattractive came. "You take care of that woman," he would direct a lesser *oficial*.

In his intelligence work, López was adept at seeking out contacts of the feminine variety. He made up in good looks what he lacked in French language ability, and he was especially effective at cocktail parties. In one case that became famous in the annals of the Paris *Centro,* he cast his eye on a good-looking lady member of the Argentine diplomatic corps in Paris. López's wife was not present at the party, and López succeeded in approaching the Argentinean and opening a conversation, and later they left together. All this in the interest of intelligence operations—or so López would claim. He sent to Havana a detailed report on the encounter, telling how he had caught the eye of the woman, how he had deftly handled a cigarette to make himself interesting to her, how she had watched him. The report went on for sixteen pages.

The official chief of the Cuban mission was Ambassador Castellanos. Castellanos' role in the Cuban revolutionary process had been limited to lending Fidel Castro a copy of the Civil Defense Code which Castro had utilized in arguing his own defense at his 1953 trial, following an abortive attempt he and his followers made to capture the military barracks in Santiago de Cuba. Castellanos assisted in defending other participants in the ill-fated assault. His personal friendship with Castro dated from those days, and with Castro in power, Castellanos was rewarded with the diplomatic plum, the ambassadorship to France. Because of his personal ties with Castro, Castellanos was more freewheeling than most Cuban envoys. He returned to Havana whenever he wished, not bothering to notify the Ministry of Foreign Affairs. Foreign Minister Raúl Roa would first learn of his trip when Castellanos would show up at the ministry.

The ambassador's friendship with Castro stood him in good stead in another way as well: Havana maintained an ample and steady flow of rum, lobsters, and cigars to the Embassy. While Cubans at home endured a severe austerity program, their ambassador in Paris was host at parties that became renowned even in that city, splendorous affairs with an abundance of good food, good liquors, and good smokes. A typical Cuban atmosphere was maintained, and the ambassador was not above taking up a pair of maracas or beating on the bongo drums. Formal receptions that were scheduled to end at ten in the evening often went on gaily until three in the morning.

The Habana-Paris Restaurant opened in the Quartier Latin, and the ambassador was a major participant in furnishing the financing for the place. The restaurant offered Cuban music and Cuban food. Certainly the latter was of the best—the ambassador provided a portion of it from the Embassy's stocks. Castellanos was the restaurant's main patron in more ways then one—almost nightly he frequented the spot until the early morning hours.

If the ambassador was not austerely revolutionary in his behavior and attitude, his wife was even less so. Blonde, good-looking, the daughter of English parents, Doris Simons Castellanos was highly intelligent and had been a professor at the University of Havana. She had little sympathy with the Cuban Revolution, and hardly bothered to display her disdain. She dressed well and enjoyed Parisian night life—and not solely with the ambassador. She made no effort to conceal her friendship with a Frenchman, a thin, myopic, balding doctor who had spent some time in Cuba and spoke Spanish well. When the ambassador was out of town, the Frenchman moved freely about the Embassy. Doris went out with him at night, returning in the early hours. When the ambassador was in residence, the trio made up an odd threesome in their outings. The ambassador and Doris were in their late forties, the French doctor about ten years younger.

Perhaps the reason the ambassador was not too concerned about his wife's doings was that he himself maintained a mistress in Havana, a woman by whom he had had one or two children. Because there frequently was friction between Castellanos and the Intelligence section, the mistress was a boon to the D.G.I. It alone knew about the ambassador's relations with her—even his wife was unaware—and D.G.I. used her as a subtle weapon of blackmail to keep Castellanos in line. The woman was virtually in the charge of D.G.I., which saw to her wants and kept the ambassador informed about her. Even if blackmail was unnecessary, the ambassador was indebted to Intelligence for keeping his secret and watching over his mistress. An *oficial* in Havana who had the code name "Janio" had responsibility for handling this matter.

Difficulties existed between Ambassador Castellanos and Intelligence because of their differing views as to the primary function of the Cuban mission. Castellanos saw the purpose of the mission to be the maintenance of good Cuban relations with France and the encouragement of trade between the two countries. López believed that the basic object of the Embassy was to carry out Intelligence operations. Castellanos feared that at some point one of these operations might cause difficulties with the French government, and this would disrupt the commerce which Cuba badly needed. One project in which he was particularly interested was the purchase of French motors which Cuba sought for cane-cutting machinery.

The Cuban mission was, in effect, a dual structure, an organization within an organization. The diplomatic functions were a shell over the intelligence operations. The chief of Intelligence reported directly to Havana; he was not accountable to the ambassador. López neither had to report to, nor take orders from, Castellanos. With the Embassy staff composed of Intelligence personnel, including the code officer and even the accountant, the control exercised by the ambassador was only nominal. (Eventually the counselor, too, was recruited by the D.G.I.) The staff did routine diplomatic work, but dropped this when intelligence tasks were pending because these always had priority. The ambassador might request a "subordinate" to do something for him, but if for any reason the *oficial* did not wish to do it, he would simply tell Castellanos, "I'll check this with López." López would decide whether the matter warranted doing. An unofficial—and only partially humorous—watchword at the Embassy was, "The illegal has precedence over the legal."

Intelligence kept a close watch on the ambassador. This was accomplished partially by means of his chauffeur, who was an *auxiliar de inteligencia.* Originally, the ambassador had a Spanish chauffeur, but he was dismissed in fear that he might be working for Spanish Intelligence or the service of another country. A new chauffeur was sent from Cuba, and it was my task to give him basic intelligence training when he arrived in Paris. Subsequently, the chauffeur kept the Intelligence section posted on the ambassador's activities. Almost daily the chauffeur provided me with a report on what Castellanos had done and where he had been the previous day: whom he had seen, what women he had been with, whether he had slept in the residence or elsewhere, whether he had been drinking heavily. I would turn the report over to López.

Later it was learned that Castellanos had fallen into disfavor with

Fidel Castro, and Intelligence learned that he waited for months for Castro to see him. It was not known whether his difficulties stemmed from his social life, his wife's activities, suspicions regarding his political reliability, or the friction with the Intelligence section.

A fundamental task with which Intelligence concerned itself was the building of a network of agents and useful contacts in Paris. The *Centro de Inteligencia* itself consisted of the *jefe*, the *segundo jefe* (Alberto Díaz Vigo, who used the code name "Duarte"), and the various *oficiales.* Everyone on the staff had outside contacts to whom he had been assigned or whom he had himself developed. All contacts had to be reported to the *Centro Principal* in Havana, and each one was placed in a category in accordance with a classification system that D.G.I. had devised for foreigners that it recruited.

The classification system had categories in ascending order of importance:

Persona de interés, person of interest: This is someone whom the Intelligence official is cultivating, with the expectation of securing a service from him later.

Vínculo útil, useful link: This is a person with whom the official is well acquainted and who has cooperated in a matter not related to intelligence.

Persona de confianza, confidential relation: A person who has displayed the proper ideological viewpoint and proved his willingness to cooperate with the Intelligence official. This person is now ready to become an

Agente, agent: An *agente* actively works with Cuban Intelligence, for pay or for ideological reasons, or perhaps as a result of a personal relationship with an *oficial.* Agents perform various functions, such as:

Agente buzón, mail drop: Receives messages from or for outside sources with whom it is inadvisable for Intelligence to be in direct communication. Sometimes this agent's house serves as a meeting place for *oficiales* and other contacts.

Agente reclutador, recruiter: Seeks contacts and agents who will be useful to Intelligence.

Agente viajero, traveler: Travels ostensibly for legitimate reasons (say as a writer or a businessman), but actually serves as a secret courier, carrying messages for Intelligence. If this

41

traveler has to make a trip to Cuba, he is provided with false documents so that his real passport and papers will show nothing to indicate that he has been there.

Agente informativo, spy: Provides Intelligence with military, diplomatic, or other governmental information.

Agente director, chief: Controls one or more other agents; in effect, he is the liaison between Intelligence and these agents. If he has several agents under him, he is the head of an espionage network.

Although these agents and contacts are neatly categorized in theory, in actuality there was, at least in Paris, rarely a clear delineation between their various activities. Their work often overlapped, as when an *agente buzón* might carry out recruiting among his acquaintances. Even espionage officials can be empire-builders, and the chief of the *Centro* in Paris, in his reports to Havana, was as likely as not to exaggerate the worth of his contacts by arbitrarily elevating their categories. This would presumably raise the importance of the chief in the eyes of Havana. In one report that he sent, López boasted of how extensively he had succeeded in penetrating the Latin American embassies in Paris. He provided the names of supposed *agentes* he had working for him in these embassies, claiming, for example, that "for penetration at the such and such embassy we now have XXX." The fact was that XXX was nothing more than a minor secretary who was being dated by a friend of a Cuban Intelligence official. Out of this vague relationship López manufactured, for purposes of his report, a full-fledged *"agente."*

VI.

Operations

I WORKED WITH A NUMBER OF CONTACTS AND AGENTS IN Paris. One of my most useful *auxiliares* was a Cuban named Nildo Alvarez Valdes (code name "Ernestico"). Alvarez was not on the D.G.I. staff, but rather was with the Cuban commercial office. Nevertheless, he served as a mail drop and contact point for Intelligence. Persons arriving in Paris who sought to get in touch with the *Centro* would contact Alvarez, who then notified Intelligence. Messages were also transmitted through Alvarez, and his house served as a meeting place, too. Persons traveling through Paris en route to Cuba occasionally stayed in Alvarez's home until passage was obtained for them. He and his wife had become accustomed to having total strangers—sometimes three or four at a time—descend on their house and remain for several days. Alvarez was about 27 years old, good-natured, balding, and rather stout. His wife chided him that his belly prevented him from seeing his toes. Alvarez's assistance was particularly convenient for me: Alvarez lived on the third floor of an apartment building at Faraday No. 10; my family lived on the fifth floor of the same building.

My tasks in Paris ranged from lesser matters, such as assisting persons who were going to Cuba, to affairs related to high policy.

For a period of time I was in contact with Paul Verges, a French deputy. Verges was trying to organize a meeting of Vietnamese, Korean, and Cuban representatives. The purpose of the conference would be to condemn the Soviet Union for not providing sufficient support to the Viet Cong and to Cuba. Fidel Castro at the time was in one of his periodic sulks against Moscow, and so the Cuban government was receptive to the idea. For a while, Intelligence, in the person of myself, encouraged Verges in his plans. The conference was to be held in Cuba or Viet Nam, and nonaligned nations were to be invited to attend. It would convene prior to the conference of Communist parties that was to meet in Moscow in 1969. The plans never came to fruition, however. Fidel Castro, although he shunned the Moscow conference, reached an agreement with the Soviets, and thus lost interest in having his own international parley.

A different type of collaboration with Cuban Intelligence was maintained by an Argentinean scientist at the National Scientific Research Center in Paris. I had carefully cultivated the Argentinean, who used the code name "Ernesto" (which seems to have had a vogue among the Intelligence collaborators in Paris). Ernesto provided detailed information about the biological research he was engaged in, as well as the work of other scientists. He also reported on the scientists themselves. Havana displayed considerable interest in Ernesto, sending precise instructions regarding the information desired from him.

On one occasion, I commented to López: "Why do they want this information? These are areas in which no work is being done in Cuba."

"Don't concern yourself," López replied. "Those are the instructions, and they have to be carried out."

I was convinced that it was not Cuban Intelligence, but rather Soviet Intelligence that was seeking the information. We Cubans were being utilized as a means of obtaining it for Moscow.

Not all efforts to build contacts in Paris had satisfactory results. A Frenchman who had been of assistance to D.G.I. in contact and recruitment work was leaving Paris to travel to Cuba. Among the Frenchman's friends was an attractive French divorcee who enjoyed the good life. E.C. worked for a publishing house and moved in intellectual circles, and Intelligence figured that she could be useful and therefore was worth remaining in contact with. This task was assigned to me. López introduced me to the Frenchman, who in turn arranged a meeting with E.C.

The Frenchman explained to E.C.: "This is a friend of mine. He's going to take care of my correspondence while I'm away. Any mail that you receive for me, please give to him."

E.C. agreed. I arranged future meetings, took her out to lunch, cultivated her; I was following the usual procedure of recruitment for Intelligence. Then, a meeting was set for nine one evening, but the woman failed to show up. I waited, then left for a secondary, "reserve" rendezvous point. No sign of E.C. here, either, so I decided to go to a reception that was being held that night at the Embassy.

At eleven o'clock E.C. appeared at the reception—obviously and thoroughly inebriated. Raucous and boisterous, she quickly became the center of amused attention at the party. López demanded to know what was going on. I explained that E.C. had failed to keep an appointment that had been set for early that evening. "*Vaya*, this is impossible," López said. "The woman can't be trusted. If that had been an important meeting, she would have done the same." Thus abruptly terminated E.C.'s relationship with Cuban Intelligence.

Then there was the case of the bizarre Brazilian. S.H., a member of the Brazilian Communist Party who had been living in exile in French Guiana, came to Paris after attending the 1967 conference of the Latin American Solidarity Organization in Cuba. He was to remain in Paris a few days, waiting for a large amount of propaganda materials that was to be sent to him from Havana, propaganda which he had promised to distribute in South America. Almost daily he showed up at the Cuban Embassy in Paris and inquired about the material, but it failed to arrive.

I came to know S.H. as a result of these visits to the Embassy. One day the Brazilian said to me, confidentially: "*Bueno*, now that I have trust in you—I see that you are honest, you are a sincere man— I have a secret to tell you."

The man was charming and seemingly intelligent, and so I, puzzled, asked, "What secret?"

"A secret that will be of great interest to the Cuban Revolution." He went on to explain that he knew of a way of securing "atomic raw materials" from which it was possible to extract cobalt. S.H. assured me that this process could be carried out in any socialist (i.e., Communist) country. He said: "I spoke to the Czechs, and they were interested, but they haven't given me a definite answer. Anyway, I would rather deal with the Cuban Revolution because it is more in need of assistance, of greater strength."

S.H.'s plan called for the smuggling of the "raw materials" from Brazil into French Guiana. S.H. told me that he was acquainted with border contrabandists, and these would be willing to do the work, despite the danger. In return for organizing the project, S.H. said he would expect ten percent of the profit, which would be used to pay the smugglers and to suborn the necessary authorities.

Propaganda supplies and nuclear raw materials were not the only matters that concerned S.H. There was also the affair of the photographs. While in Havana, the Brazilian had been wont to leave the organized, guided groups to which he was assigned and go off by himself. He had a borrowed car and a borrowed camera, and he took photographs on his one-man sight-seeing excursions. This had not pleased the Cuban authorities. When it had come time to leave—so S.H. related to me—he had wanted to keep his film. At the airport he approached what he took to be a representative of the Cuban Institute for Friendship with the Peoples and said to him: "This camera was loaned by your Institute, and I want to give it back. I don't know how to remove the cartridge. Will you please do it for me? "

The man agreed, took the camera, and returned shortly afterwards and handed S.H. a cartridge. In Paris, S.H. took the cartridge to a photo shop for developing. When he went back five days later to pick up the developed photographs, the clerk demanded to know whether this was some kind of a joke—the cartridge had been empty, there was no film in it. S.H. realized that the film had been removed by the man at the airport, who evidently had been D.G.I. or G-2.

I dispatched a message about S.H. to the *Centro Principal* in Havana, relating the offer he had made about nuclear materials. A reply came back from the official in charge of Brazilian affairs, "Fermín," who reported that D.G.I. had been in touch with S.H. in Cuba, but that he never said anything about atomic secrets, nor offered anything. Perhaps he was trying to work a swindle, or he was an enemy provoker, or maybe just plain crazy. I was ordered not to have anything further to do with him, and I never saw him again.

A fundamental task of the Intelligence Center in Paris was to provide support for the various guerrilla movements the Cuban government was attempting to spawn in Latin America. Of the Latin

American republics, only Mexico maintained diplomatic and commercial ties with Cuba—and Mexican surveillance of Cuban intelligence activities in that country was brisk. With no direct means of commercial transportation existing between Cuba and the other Latin American countries, it was difficult for Cuba to move men back and forth. Latin Americans received guerrilla training in Cuba, and then Cuba would utilize its fleet of Lambda-type fishing boats to smuggle the men, together with weapons, back into their home countries. To get people from these countries to Cuba—for training or other purposes—was more difficult. A regular schedule of clandestine pickups was not feasible.

Thus, the Paris *Centro* entered the picture. Persons traveling to Cuba from Latin America would fly to Paris on any of the several commercial air routes operating to Europe. They would remain in Paris while the *Centro* obtained the necessary documentation for further travel, either Russian or Czech visas. From Paris, the men would fly to Moscow or Prague, and from there to Havana on Soviet TU-114 airliners.

One week a group of Bolivians arrived in Paris. Another week a group of Argentineans. Then Venezuelans. Each *oficial* at the *Centro* dealt with specific countries, and Venezuelan matters were my concern. A typical case was that of the Cruz brothers, one about 22 years old, the other a bit older. The usual message was received at the *Centro*: Persons of such-and-such description will arrive in Paris. They will contact Ernesto. Arrange for their travel requirements.

Travelers of this type were not met at the airport, so as not to reveal official Cuban interest in them. They would phone an *agente buzón* upon their arrival, and then proceed to whatever address he directed them. The *agente* would notify the *Centro* that the men had arrived, and then one of the officials would go to see them and arrange for their continued travel. The *Centro* was rarely told much about the men: the reasons for their travel and sometimes even their true nationality was usually not divulged, either by Havana or by the men themselves.

The Cruz brothers arrived in Paris toward the end of 1968. I was assigned to take care of them, and I went to see them at Alvarez's house, where they were staying, in order to ascertain their requirements and obtain data to be used in securing Czech visas. The two men were willing to talk, and I learned that they had been with

47

guerrillas in Venezuela for three years. Their view of the revolutionary situation in that country was bleakly pessimistic: the guerrillas had made no progress, they were receiving no popular support, and because of internal dissension they had split into factional groups.

I was surprised at the Cruzes' attitude toward Douglas Bravo, a Venezuelan guerrilla leader who had received a large amount of laudatory publicity in the Cuban press. They said that Bravo had spent little time in the mountains, and not done much fighting, preferring to remain hidden in the cities. Bravo, the Cruzes reported, had gone up into the mountains on one occasion when a group of Cubans and Venezuelans was infiltrated from Cuba. "The Cubans identified themselves, gave their names and ranks, only to Bravo," the Cruzes related. "But the next day everyone in camp knew this information. Bravo talked too much."

The effort by Cuba's Ernesto Guevara to develop a guerrilla movement in Bolivia is now a matter of history. It is also well-known that Guevara envisioned "two, three or many Viet Nams" in the hemisphere. What has not previously been revealed is that, in order to achieve this goal, Cuba planned a two-pronged attack on South America. The first prong was to emanate from Bolivia, the second from Venezuela. Guevara was not the only high-ranking representative of the Castro regime involved right on the scene of action. At approximately the time Guevara was preparing to go to Bolivia, two members of the Central Committee of the Cuban Communist Party were infiltrated into Venezuela to assist the guerrillas operating there. The Cubans were Raúl Menendez Tomassevich and Orestes Guerra González, both of them *comandantes*, highest rank in the Cuban Army.

The two officers came through Paris separately in 1968 en route back to Cuba. They were tired, in poor physical shape, and altogether disillusioned about the Venezuelan effort. Tomassevich was the first to come to Paris, arriving in the summer. Because of his rank, he was in the charge of the ambassador, although I had an opportunity to chat with him. Our acquaintanceship dated from an odd circumstance: in Havana, we both had patronized the same shooting gallery on the Prado. Tomassevich spoke of his disappointment with the Venezuelans, and told of a problem much like that encountered by Guevara in Bolivia. The Venezuelans distrusted Tomassevich precisely because of his high rank, believing that he was not there to help them, but rather to take command of the guerrilla movement. "They would not believe that we Cubans had come only to fight as soldiers," Tomassevich complained. "Nothing progressed. Always there were the misgivings, the fears that the Cubans were going to take over."

Tomassevich was in Paris two days, after which the ambassador took him to Prague, and from there he returned to Cuba. Tomassevich was about 44 years old, but during the approximately three years spent in Venezuela he had aged considerably. He was noticeably ill, and whereas in Cuba he had weighed about 180 pounds, his weight was now down to about 130. He arrived in Havana in such poor shape that when Raúl Castro saw him he conceived one of his macabre jokes: he would announce Tomassevich's death, put him in a coffin, and let other officers file by to pay their last respects. Raúl later thought better of the idea, and did not go through with it.

Orestes Guerra came to Paris after Tomassevich. Guerra also spoke of the unfavorable state of the Venezuelan guerrillas: hungry, in hiding, out of contact with the urban clandestine movements. The guerrillas had good weapons, but they were not using them, they were not fighting. There were bitter divisions, with different groups following different leaders. There was resentment against the Cubans, and in one case a small Cuban-Venezuelan group had set itself up independently under a Cuban who used the name "Antonio."

Guerra placed the blame for the guerrilla failure on a number of factors. He talked of new policies by the Venezuelan government, which had eased repressive measures and offered leniency to guerrillas who surrendered. At the same time, however, there had been determined pursuit by the Venezuelan army of those guerrillas who chose to remain in the hills. Guerra found much fault with Douglas Bravo, saying: "He's the national leader of the revolutionary youth of Venezuela, but he has betrayed the goals of the Revolution. He has never actively participated in the guerrilla war, although he became famous as a guerrilla, as if he were always fighting. He lives in the city, and he only goes up into the mountains in order to get money when it is sent from Cuba, or to issue instructions." Guerra was particularly indignant because of the belief among the guerrillas that Bravo had gone capitalist and purchased a factory and an apartment house—presumably with the funds sent from Cuba for fomenting revolution. (The reports on these matters presumably made in

49

Havana by Tomassevich and Guerra may well have been the reason for the drop-off in Cuban aid to Venezuelan guerrillas which seems to have occurred in 1969.)

Guerra and another Cuban who had accompanied him from Venezuela were in my charge. I flew with them to Prague, and there turned them over to the chief of the Cuban Intelligence Center in that city. From Prague they would proceed home, via Moscow.

One of the mysteries of the Cold War was the disappearance of Colonel Francisco Alberto Caamaño Deñó. Caamaño had been the military commander of the rebels in the 1965 uprising in the Dominican Republic. Subsequently, as part of a political settlement, he was sent to London to serve there as Dominican military attache. In October 1967 he made a trip to The Hague—and disappeared.

In Paris, I received instructions to carry out a detailed survey of a section of the city where a meeting of two important persons could be held, free of possible surveillance by French Counter-Intelligence. I was told that one of the individuals was "Armando," a D.G.I. official in Havana who had directed the Cuban end of the Guevara operation in Bolivia. Later I learned that the second person was Caamaño.

I studied a route which Caamaño could follow in Paris, along which D.G.I. officials would be spaced in order to guard him. The actual meeting with Armando would take place at a café.

On the appointed day, the plan worked perfectly. Caamaño dressed in mufti and wearing a toupee that didn't quite match the rest of his hair, walked along the prearranged streets under the watchful eyes of the *oficiales*. I was the final official at the end of the route, near the café meeting place. I saw that Caamaño did not appear to be followed, and the meeting was held without incident.

A few days later I had occasion to go to Prague, and in that city I stayed in a "safe" apartment used by D.G.I. I found that Caamaño and Armando were also there, preparing to go to Cuba. Clearly Caamaño was to participate in a new Cuban subversive plan, probably one directed at the Dominican Republic. It may well be that Fidel Castro envisioned building Caamaño into a second Guevara.

Before leaving Cuba, as preparation for my duty abroad, I had been briefed on how to spot possible surveillance by French Counter-Intelligence and how to try to evade it. When I arrived in Paris, however, I found that the French did not appear interested in the

Centro and posed ι. particular problem. This was a matter of some disappointment to ιne *Centro* officials: "The French are not checking on us; they don't follow us. They don't think we're important."

As it turned out, the French did not leave the Cubans in permanent limbo. One day Roberto Alvarez Barrera (code name "Remigio"), a fellow official at the *Centro,* came to me and said, "Am I seeing phantoms, or am I being followed? " The earlier officials at the *Centro* had not received specialized training in such matters as the tailing of people, as I had been given. I went walking with Alvarez, and was able to ascertain that Alvarez was indeed being followed. This was reported to Havana, and the *Centro Principal* ordered that a detailed study was to be made of the surveillance. I went to work watching the watchers: I noted the individuals involved, what they wore, how well they operated, the cars utilized, whether license plates were switched. I also noted where the French usually parked their surveillance vehicles, as well as where men who were afoot stood waiting. I would watch Alvarez when he left the Embassy, and sometimes I would watch from his fifth-floor apartment, observing whatever cars followed Alvarez as, by prearrangement, he drove by in the street below.

Alvarez, one of the sharper *oficiales,* had two fondnesses: he liked to dress well and he enjoyed good music. He would ask me to accompany him on his shopping excursions for suits and records. The French persisted in their surveillance, and Alvarez would rarely go out alone. He became fearful that he might be kidnapped or an attempt made to kill him. He knew that he was of special interest to the French because he had been in contact with one of the student leaders in the riots that had wracked Paris that May.

On one occasion I went out with Alvarez, but left him afterwards in order to go to a bookstore. I noticed a young man, blond, bespectacled, staring into store windows—despite the considerable cold of that day. I stayed in the bookstore for a period of time, and then the man sauntered in and looked around. Later I spotted the same person in one of the vehicles I knew was used by French Counter-Intelligence.

If the French were hoping to pressure Alvarez into leaving the country, they succeeded in their design. Havana, apparently figuring he was of no further utility in Paris, recalled him home.

French interest in the *Centro* fluctuated. At times the officials were able to detect no surveillance; at other times it was intense. Two types of street surveillance were used. In one method, the person or persons doing the tailing sought to avoid detection by remaining as inconspicuous as possible. In the second method, the surveillance was carried out by several cars and persons afoot, and there was no attempt at concealment. This method intended that the person who was being tailed know that he was under close watch, and it was usually aimed at limiting that person's activities. (The Cubans called this type of tailing *japonesa*—perhaps the Japanese like to utilize it.) I found that in evading surveillance, the great and unruly Parisian traffic was my best ally. I could lose myself among the many vehicles, and the most skillful of tails was unable to follow me.

I became convinced that the French were not unduly concerned about the activities of the *Centro*, except as these pertained directly to French affairs. The French kept watch, not only by surveillance and probably by wiretapping and electronic eavesdropping, but also through the utilization of some of the *Centro's* own contacts as double-agents. Most of the Cuban staff were poorly trained, or not trained at all; they committed errors. After they had been in Paris a while they became too confident and tended to underestimate Counter-Intelligence, and often did not take proper security precautions.

The Cubans overlooked a vital fact: They were comparatively new at the game. The French had been at it for centuries.

VII.

Guevara

ERNESTO "CHE" GUEVARA, THE RESTLESS REVOLUTION-
ary from Argentina, joined Fidel Castro in Mexico in the mid-fifties,
and from then on Guevara's star was in the ascendancy. Eventually
he would become one of the most colorful lights in the Communist
galaxy.

Guevara's activities during a turbulent ten years have been fully
recorded, by himself as well as by others: the expedition to Cuba,
the struggle in the Sierra Maestra, final victory, and then the many
positions Guevara occupied in the new Castro regime. But after this
came mystery, a period of two years when Guevara slipped completely from public sight. Guevara had made a lengthy trip which
carried him from the United Nations to Africa, to Europe, to Asia,
and then back to Cuba—where he promptly disappeared. Historians,
newspapermen, and intelligence agents have delved into the puzzle,
but as yet only partial fragments have come to light.

In Paris, I was able to learn some of the missing pieces of information, details regarding Guevara's ill-fated attempt to lead a guerrilla
war in Africa, and his later, final adventure in Bolivia. That Guevara
had secretly returned to Africa after his previous, well-publicized
trip was first learned when Ciro Roberto Bustos, an Angentinian

who joined Guevara in Bolivia and was later captured by Bolivian troops, made a detailed statement to Bolivian Intelligence which included the gists of conversations Bustos had had with Guevara. Guevara had believed, according to Bustos, that revolutions could be engendered in

> ... Africa and South America, with the advantage in favor of Africa because of its greater distance from the United States and its greater logistic possibilities (Soviet Union, China, United Arab Republic, Algeria). During his extensive voyage through Africa and Asia before disappearing from Cuba, Guevara arranged for his incorporation in the struggle in the Congo, that is, he chose Africa. But the experience turned out to be negative, because, he said, the human element failed. . .

What had happened in Africa?

One of the collaborators with Cuban Intelligence in Paris was a Cuban doctor, Rodrigo Alvarez Cambra (who used the nickname "Kiko"). Cambra had obtained a scholarship for advanced studies in his field, orthopedics, and spent about a year in Paris, during which time his intelligence tasks consisted primarily of working among university students. Cambra visited the chancellery for romantic as well as professional reasons: he was dating a French girl, Anik, employed there as a secretary and translator.

Cambra had been in the Congo with Guevara, and in conversations with me he revealed what had happened there. For Guevara and a group of Cubans who were with him this had been an odyssey of frustration. They had endured severe privations, and little had been accomplished. Rather than leading a guerrilla campaign, they found themselves giving their African allies rudimentary military training, and when not occupied thus, they were busy trying to keep the tribes from fighting among themselves.

In one combat, Cambra related, a Cuban and several Africans were killed, and a number of Guevara's African allies had fled in terror. Later the tribesmen who had not retreated demanded that the others drink the blood of slain enemies in order to regain their lost valor. For good measure, the Cubans were expected to do likewise, and this they refused to do.

There were angry arguments, and the tribe that was expected to drink blood rebelled outright. Guevara and his Cubans had to flee

54

through the jungles, pursued by enemy troops and their former allies. It took them a month to get to safety, and Guevara remarked in disgust that it would be another hundred years before the Africans would be ready to receive help in winning their "liberation."

Cambra revealed that the Russians had been against Guevara's African adventure, warning that the Africans were not yet sufficiently developed for a movement of this type. Fidel Castro had not agreed, and there had been friction between him and the Russians over the matter. As it turned out, events proved the Russians to be right, and the affair ended in a near-farcical fiasco.

Guevara eventually slipped back into Cuba, there to prepare his Bolivian adventure—he was now accepting his second choice of a target area, since Africa had failed. Toward the end of 1967 he secretly entered Bolivia, and there launched a new guerrilla movement. Despite initial successes, the guerrillas soon suffered setbacks because of the lack of cooperation of the local peasantry and persistent pursuit by the Bolivian army.

The Intelligence *Centro* in Paris performed a support role for Guevara. While he was in Africa, groups of eight to twelve soldiers would arrive periodically in Paris from Cuba. All were Cuban Negroes, and the *Centro* had to find hotel accommodations for them before they could be sent to Africa. Their rugged appearance caused French eyebrows to be lifted, particularly in view of their pose as "technicians" and other "professional" people. Even after Guevara's adventure had ended, Cuban Negro soldiers were still being sent to Africa as Castro persisted in attempting to establish his influence there. A substantial Cuban military mission was accepted and set up at Brazzaville.

The Paris *Centro* continued to lend support when Guevara was in Bolivia. Isolated as he was in the Bolivian jungles, Guevara had difficulty in communicating with Havana. This problem was partially solved by having Guevara send written messages to an *agente buzón* in Paris, who then turned them over to the *Centro*. These messages were transmitted in sealed envelopes. From Paris the envelopes, still unopened, were dispatched by courier to Havana, where they were subjected to laboratory tests to find out whether they might have been tampered with at any point in their long journey.

A major service performed for Guevara by the *Centro* was the recruitment of a writer to go to Bolivia to gather material for what was to have been the first public revelation of Guevara's presence in that country. Havana had requested that a trustworthy and ideologically suitable writer be found, and to this end López, the chief of the *Centro,* contacted Francois Maspero, a French editor and publisher with whom Intelligence had had dealings. Maspero, in turn, put López in contact with Régis Debray, a French writer of lesser note. A number of conversations ensued, and López succeeded in recruiting Debray for the task. López, in talking to me, described Debray as impulsive, determined, highly cooperative, and "considers himself very brave." Debray was sent to Cuba, and from there he made his way to Bolivia and Guevara's guerrilla encampment. But romantic dreams in Paris did not jibe with the realities of a harsh bush existence in Bolivia, and Debray was soon eager to leave the guerrillas. He did so, was captured, brought to trial, and given a thirty-year prison sentence.

Cuban Intelligence did not lose interest in Debray. In Paris, the *Centro* continued to maintain contact with his mother.

Guevara's Bolivian effort ended in complete failure. Guevara and the remnants of his group were tracked down, and Guevara was taken prisoner and shortly afterwards executed. The story did not end there, however, for the Intelligence Center in Paris. Guevara had kept a daily diary in Bolivia, and this had been captured by the Bolivian army. Newspapermen and publishers' representatives from around the world sought to buy or otherwise obtain copies of the diary, but the Bolivian High Command delayed in reaching a decision on this—and then a startling event occurred. Fidel Castro announced that Cuba had secured a copy of the diary and was publishing and releasing it for worldwide distribution.

How had Cuba obtained the diary? It was soon revealed that a copy had been sent to Cuba by a most unlikely person, Antonio Arguedas, Minister of the Interior in the Bolivian government, who as head of the Bolivian police had played a major role in breaking up the clandestine apparatus which was to have provided support for Guevara's guerrillas. Had Arguedas been a Castro agent all along? The answer seems to be no, for the Cuban government appears to have been as surprised by his actions as were the Bolivians. The *Centro Principal* of Intelligence in Cuba sent an urgent message to the *Centro* in Paris instructing it to send two officials to make contact with Arguedas, who had fled to Chile. These officials were to find out if

56

Arguedas wanted to go to Cuba, and if so, to assist him in getting there. They were also to ascertain whether he had any additional documents he wished to turn over to the Cuban government.

Roberto Alvares Barrera (code name "Remigio") and I were selected to go to Chile. Ambassador Castellanos, who maintained friendly relations with other Latin American diplomats in Paris, was requested to obtain Chilean visas for us and this he accomplished promptly. The person we were instructed to contact for assistance in Chile was a sympathizer toward the Cuban Revolution, Senator Salvador Allende, now president of Chile. Just as we were about to depart, a new message from Havana called the whole thing off. Arguedas was talking wildly, and Intelligence now thought better of trying to contact him.

One last chapter of the Guevara affair remained. Three Cubans survived Guevara's final battle with the Bolivian Rangers who had been pursuing him. Realizing that further fighting was futile—"This is finished" they said—they had decided to flee rather than risk their lives further. In Chile, Senator Allende sent a number of Bolivian scouts fanning out to see if they could make contact with any guerrilla survivors. Two of these guides eventually found the three Cubans and began guiding them to Chile.

The group encountered Guido ("Inti") Peredo Leigue, who had been the Bolivian guerrilla chieftain under Guevara. Peredo was also fleeing, and he demanded the right to get to Chile first, with the Cubans to follow later. The Cubans heatedly stated that they were foreigners who had come to fight for Bolivia, and it was their prerogative to leave first, and that at any rate Peredo could wait because he knew the land better. The Cubans continued on their journey, prepared to battle with Peredo if he attempted to stop them. Thus ended ignominiously the comradeship Guevara had sought to develop between Bolivians and Cubans. (The following year Peredo was killed by Bolivian police.)

Before reaching the Chilean frontier, the Cubans and their two Bolivian guides arrived at a town frequented by border smugglers. They sought food and rest, and were taken to the home of a local official, who greeted them in apparent friendship. They realized, however, that he was setting a trap to capture them. To make their escape they had to shoot their way out of the town. As they were leaving they heard Bolivian transport planes circling overhead, presumably carrying paratroopers. The troops were evidently unable to jump because of the night darkness.

Once into Chile the five men hid in a cave, where they listened to a transistor radio they had somehow obtained along the way. When news reports convinced them that Chile would not be hostile to them, they surrendered to the Chilean authorities. The men were granted safe-conduct to leave the country. Havana contacted its Embassy in Paris, which made arrangements for the five men to fly to Tahiti and then to Paris. The French acquiesced to this provided that the Cubans made no public statements while on French soil.

Ambassador Castellanos and the second in command of the Intelligence *Centro*, Alberto Díaz Vigo (who doubled as consul), flew to Tahiti to meet the guerrillas and escort them to Paris. I was among the Cuban officials who greeted them at Le Bourget Airport and took them to Orly Airport, from whence they flew on to Prague, Moscow, and Havana. In conversing with the men, I learned the details of their escape and obtained new insights into the Guevara affair in Bolivia. For one thing, I was told, Bolivia had never been Guevara's primary goal. He had planned to use it merely as a springboard. From Bolivia the guerrilla movement was to have fanned out into adjoining countries, creating what Guevara hoped would become "two, three, or many Viet Nams" in the Western Hemisphere.

One of the reasons the guerrilla movement floundered was that it failed to receive expected reinforcements. Additional men trained in Cuba were to join Guevara, but upon arriving in La Paz they would meet with Mario Monje, a Bolivian Communist leader who had broken with Guevara over the issue of Cuban as against Bolivian leadership of the guerrillas. Monje, I was told by the Guevara survivors, would inform the new arrivals that the movement was "a disaster, a failure," that they would not be able to reach the guerrillas. He would convince them to turn back.

There has been puzzlement as to why Guevara persisted in remaining in Bolivia when it became evident that his group faced inevitable defeat and destruction. The survivors revealed that this was not so, that actually Guevara had decided to leave Bolivia. He remained those final—and what proved to be fatal—days because he was attempting to locate a guerrilla remnant that had become separated from the main body, and which he did not want to abandon. (Guevara was unaware that that group had already been wiped out by the Bolivian army.)

The Ernesto Guevara of those last, desperate days was not the flashing figure of legendary fame. He was "wasted physically, totally destroyed," according to the survivors. Realizing that defeat was imminent, "everything bothered him, exasperated him—he had a temper of all the devils upon him." Not only had Guevara suffered decisive military defeat; worse, his hopes had evaporated and his dreams forsaken him. The long and arduous road he had chosen to travel had ended in complete failure.

There was a footnote to the story of the Paris *Centro* and Guevara. Months after Cambra, the doctor who had been with him in Africa, returned to Havana from Paris, a German lady came to the Cuban Embassy. A secretary inquired of her, "What do you wish? "

"I am the wife of Dr. Alvarez Cambra," the woman answered, "and I want to ask about him, I want to see him." She was clearly in an advanced state of pregnancy.

The secretary informed me, and I then spoke to the woman, asking her again what she wanted. She repeated impatiently, "I am Dr. Cambra's wife, and I haven't heard from him in two or three months, and I want to see him."

I told her that Cambra had returned to Cuba, whereupon she staged an emotional scene, crying that she had been abandoned. I later learned that the woman had obtained travel papers and had gone to Cuba to seek Cambra. This led to amused speculation in the Intelligence section: the staff knew that Cambra already had one wife in Cuba.

Russia

THE ALLIANCE BETWEEN FIDEL CASTRO AND THE SOVIET Union has been one of the continuing hot spots of the Cold War. Soviet support for Cuba permitted the latter country to carry out a program of subversion which, at one time or another, affected virtually every country in Latin America. In 1962 the alliance almost plunged the world into a nuclear conflagration.

The alliance, however, has not been a happy one. Born not of kinship and probably little conviction, the Havana-Moscow axis grew out of necessity and adventurism—Castro's necessity and Russia's adventurism. Faced with increasing United States resentment and resistance to his programs—including mass executions, widespread expropriations, and grandiose aspirations to hemispheric leadership—Castro moved into the arms of the Russian bear. Then, when invasion ships were approaching Cuban shores in 1961, Castro declared, "The Revolution is socialist," and he hastily accepted comradeship with the Soviet Union.

When one dances with the bear, one finds that the embrace grows tighter. Castro chafed in the embrace and tried to maintain his independence. The Russians felt that since they were supporting him, he should be properly subservient. Castro resisted, and Moscow attempted to maneuver old-line Cuban Communists into dominant positions, thus hoping to diminish and perhaps eventually destroy Castro's power. Castro, however, met the challenges head-on, cracked down on the Moscow followers, even brought some to trial and sent them to prison.

In the Soviet Union Nikita Krushchev was thrown out of power, and the hard-nosed bureaucrats who took over were not of the kind to tolerate indiscipline on the part of Castro, whom they viewed as a mere puppet, and a highly dependent one, at that.

Because Cuba was not capable of supporting itself economically, nor of obtaining in foreign trade all the goods it needed, a supply lifeline from the Soviet Union to the island had been established. Vital to Cuban existence was the petroleum that Russia kept flowing aboard a steady stream of tankers. The Kremlin hardened its position toward Castro, and the flow of petroleum was slowed. The Cuban economy found itself in grievous trouble. There was not enough fuel to keep sugar mills, industries, and vehicles functioning. In a desperate move, military chief Raúl Castro allocated about one-third of military fuel stockpiles to civilian use. Other supplies from Russia on which Cuba was dependent also failed to arrive, forcing closure of a number of factories. Their workers were sent to toil in the cane fields.

In February 1969, the chief of the Cuban Intelligence Center in Paris, Armando López, summoned his *oficiales* to a meeting. He was just back from a trip to Havana, where he had conferred with D.G.I. chief Piñeiro.* López gravely announced, "*Somos más soviéticos*" ("We are more Soviet"). The Castro government had bowed under the Russian pressure, and a secret agreement had been reached between the two governments. López, at this meeting and in subsequent conversations, revealed the general terms of the accord. He

---

*López was a personal friend of Piñeiro, and he had accompanied Piñeiro and Raúl Castro on a hunting trip. During this trip, Raúl related how the decision was made for the Soviet Union to send nuclear missiles to Cuba. Raúl had at the time been in Moscow conferring with Khrushchev, and had requested weapons assistance from the Soviet Union. During the conversation Khrushchev suddenly hit the table with his fist and declared, "What is more, I am going to give you offensive weapons also, because if you are attacked, then you have a right to attack and defend yourselves." Cuba, according to Raúl, had not requested offensive weapons. Khrushchev had offered them, stipulating only that they remain under Soviet control.

cautioned us that we were not to tell even our wives about the agreement.

A few years earlier, when the Castro star had been in the ascendancy in Latin America, the Soviet Union had had little choice but to go along with his plans, policies, and postures. A vast program of subversion and guerrilla warfare was prepared in Cuba and supported from there, causing considerable trouble for Latin America. The plans repeatedly failed, however, and as the years went by, it became evident that Castro's overall policy was a failure, too: not a single country fell to communism. Castro had lost his luster, his efforts had led to naught, and so Russia began to diverge from the Cuban line and to return to its old policy of the *vía pacífica.* Respectability was to be the keynote: Moscow would seek friendly relations with the Latin American governments, and the Moscow-dominated Communist parties would forsake subversion for old-fashioned politicking.

Castro had been most unhappy about the Soviet attitude, and had expressed his displeasure publicly. Now, however, this outspokenness was over. As part of the Cuban-Soviet agreement, Castro would refrain from criticizing the, Soviet Union and its foreign policies. Castro would also cease attacking the old-time Communist parties of Latin America that did not follow his subversive line. In effect, Moscow would pursue its own policies in Latin America, free of criticism or interference by Castro.

The Soviet Union, as its part of the agreement, would provide Cuba with the economic support that it needed. That assistance has been estimated at some $350,000,000 worth of petroleum and goods annually. Russia promised to increase the quantity of raw materials and agricultural machinery it was sending to Cuba, as well as to enlarge its purchases of Cuban products.

A significant part of the Cuban-Soviet accord called for the sending of approximately 5,000 technicians to Cuba. There had been a substantial number of Soviet specialists in Cuba previously, but many of these had been withdrawn when relations between the two countries had deteriorated. Now the technicians would come back, and they would work in the agricultural, mining, fishing, and atomic energy fields, as well as with the Cuban military and intelligence services. The Soviets were particularly interested in expanding Cuban production of nickel, a raw material needed by the Soviets. In the atomic field, Russia would provide Cuba with an experimental nuclear power plant.

Whereas on the surface it appeared that the Soviet technicians would be serving only in advisory capacities, it was apparent, from their large number as well as from the circumstances of the Havana-Moscow agreement, that in many cases their role would shift from advisory to supervisory, semantically disguised as this might be. The Soviet Union had finally succeeded in tightening its hold on maverick Castro.

One payoff for the Russians came at the time of their invasion of Czechoslovakia. Castro was one of the few Communist figures outside Russia who publicly supported the Soviet move.

In the intelligence field, new advisers would be assigned to the D.G.I. They would also serve as liaison officers between D.G.I. and the Soviet intelligence service, the K.G.B. (Komitet Gosudarstvennoi Bezopasnosti—Committee for State Security). For, under terms of the agreement, the operations of the D.G.I. would thereafter be more closely coordinated with those of the K.G.B. D.G.I. virtually became an arm of Soviet Intelligence—a fact of special value to Russia in regard to operations in the United States, where D.G.I. had been utilizing the stream of Cuban refugees as a cover for the infiltration of agents.

Over a period of years, the Soviet Union provided Cuba with most of its military equipment, and this had made the Cuban Army the most powerful in Latin America. As a result of the new Cuban-Soviet agreement, Russia began re-equipping Castro's forces with everything from routine gear to new types of surface-to-air guided missiles. These latter were more accurate and had longer ranges than those previously emplaced on the island. The military importance of Cuba to the Soviet Union was made plain by the visit to Havana in July 1969 of a flotilla of Soviet warships, and the visit in November of the same year of Soviet Defense Minister Andrei A. Grechko. Subsequently, additional Soviet warships have visited Cuban ports, and long-range Soviet military aircraft have flown in and out of Cuban airfields.

The secret Soviet-Cuban pact culminated in the construction of a base for Soviet nuclear submarines in the port of Cienfuegos. The use of this base would greatly increase the operational capabilities of Soviet submarines in the Atlantic.

In an interview published by the Soviet newspaper *Isvestia* early in 1970, Raúl Castro was quoted as saying: "We have learned a lot in the past. We have matured. Therefore, we believe that the possibilities for friendship and cooperation between Cuba and the Soviet Union are now more positive."

It was another way of saying, We were wrong, they are right. The Soviet Union, clearly, was now the boss. Cuba was now indeed ominously more Sovietic.

IX.

Decision

TO DEFECT IS TO ALTER DRASTICALLY ONE'S WHOLE LIFE, and the lives of all members of the family. To defect is not merely to abandon an ideology, or to exchange one ideology for another. To defect is to forsake one's entire past, country, friends; to cast aside memories, background, associations. The decision to leave is a tortuous one; it is reached only after great soul searching and examination of realities. There is not only the act of leaving. There is also the facing of innumerable uncertainties, the seeking of a new life—and what will that new life be?

My decision to defect was rooted in the very Revolution for which I had fought. The seeds were planted over a period of years; they grew and blossomed in Paris. Revolutions devour their sons; they can also betray them. Probably most Cubans sympathized with the Cuban Revolution in its initial stages; a great many turned against it when it changed course from freedom to communism and demagoguery and dictatorship.

I took part in the July 26 Revolution, but never with foreign ideologies in mind, communism, all that about proletarian internationalism. As I developed with the Revolution, I watched the revolutionary process. While I fought in the Escambray and at Girón

Beach, I was never the fanatic who did things because he was told to do them and without seeing the realities of the matter. Friends of mine, some of them not in sympathy with the Revolution, told me of arbitrary acts that had been committed within the revolutionary process, and at first I thought that these acts were the fault of extremists, extremists who had managed to get into the Revolution. But as the Revolution proceeded and these things continued, I came to realize that they were more widespread, that they were part of the process itself. There was the mistreatment of those persons who criticized the Revolution, who saw that it was changing in character, that it was betraying the principles for which it had been fought. It was said that those who were critical were "foreign" elements, perhaps recruited by foreign intelligence. If you had opinions contrary to those held by Fidel, that was enough to label you as belonging to the C.I.A., as being counterrevolutionary. You then were no longer treated as a human being, but as a political enemy; you were an undesirable, a person who had to be cast off. Such a person had to be separated, he must not be dealt with, and anyone who did treat with him was viewed as a weak revolutionary, as perhaps someone who was himself suspect.

All that humbug, all those lies, all those promises that Fidel made, to elevate the level of life, to work for the social good—I remembered those promises. Whenever he would say such-and-such will be carried out in thus-and-thus time, I would remember, and when it wasn't carried out, I knew this had been a hoax. They were lies, all that about raising the standards of the peasantry to that of the cities, making the differences between field and city disappear. As I came to know and understand these demagogic plans, and saw that they were not being fulfilled, I knew that the failures were not due to counterrevolution, upon which the blame was placed. The faults were within the system itself. I was a part of the revolutionary process and I saw that the defects were inside, within itself, a sickness of the system, and not the fault of "foreign elements."

During 1962—the year of the missile crisis—with the blockade in effect against Cuba, even the most basic commodities became scarce. The government mobilized thousands and thousands of workers to do "voluntary" work in the fields in order to harvest the cane crop and other crops. Although at times this mass labor had ill results—as when amateur cutters damaged the cane—the general effect was very good, and the food level could have been raised. We were told that all that effort, that sacrifice, the product of all that work, would be used to benefit the entire people. But then we saw that it was not used to help the people, there was an unmerciful policy of exportation, ninety percent of the products were sent abroad, without heed to the fact that the Cuban people had to eat, had to have clothing. There were restrictions, rationing, and calls to more sacrifice, and there were proclamations of immense rewards to follow, great results for the people, a marvelous future. I began to understand that all this was part of the international Communist system, that this was the only way the people could be kept working. Their hopes must always be maintained.

I became disillusioned; there were disappointments and disappointments. There would be announcements of gains made by the peasants, and when I went out into the fields I saw the *campesinos*, and they were more hungry, their clothes more tattered, and there was no clear future for them. I could see the great deception that was being carried out by communism.

The reality was completely different than the reports that were given. The Cuban magazines, the publications sent abroad, told of the achievements of the Revolution as if these benefited the Cuban people. Propaganda went out to Latin America, to the entire world, aimed at presenting the Cuban Revolution as something magnificent, different than revolutionary processes that had occurred in other places.

There was that famous Agrarian Reform. The government pompously announced that the lands would be broken up and distributed, or would be used to benefit all the people. There was much propaganda about this. Books were published, and these became a catechism for revolutionaries. All the means of diffusion in Cuba told about the Agrarian Reform, this was one of the most altruistic measures of the Revolution, this was a tremendous good. But then the government took the land, the *campesino* was forced to sell; he was held by the neck, the land was seized, there was no more propaganda, nothing was said, nothing was printed.

I was part of the system, even though I saw these problems. Perhaps it was opportunism. Many of us who had fought for something different—now we were not interested in any of these questions, we had fought and won and wanted to enjoy, we wanted to rise within the system, to acquire positions of importance without concerning ourselves about the misfortunes of the people.

Did I want my children to grow up in such a society? Norma and I now had two boys (one of them born in Paris). I wanted them to respect their nation, to respect me, too.

When comes the awakening of the conscience? Friends of mine had been imprisoned, their lands arbitrarily seized. They were good people, honorable, and all their lives they had done honest labor.

I knew that I was an instrument of the system, of that monstrosity, of that deception. I was in it not because of fanaticism, but because I was carried along and did not resist, and so I could not close my eyes to what was there, to occurrences that I did not like, defects that were apparent, bad things that I saw. By the time I was preparing to go to Paris, it was probably in my subconscious that I would break with the Revolution. Then, in Paris, there were these officials who personified all the deceit, all the falsities of the Revolution, men who only wanted to keep climbing, who didn't care a fig about the calamities of the people. They were blind, or made themselves blind, to reality.

Which is the drop that overflows the cup? In the fall of 1968 a plan was announced at the Paris Embassy for the setting up of a *círculo infantil* for the children of the staff. Instead of attending French schools, the children would study and play at the *círculo*, where they would receive a proper revolutionary education. The wives of the Embassy personnel would work at the *círculo*.

The plan was pushed by a militant Cuban woman, Cordelia Navarro, who was attached to UNESCO and was in Paris on a visit. Navarro called a meeting of the staff wives and told them that the running of the *círculo* would provide them with a worthwhile "revolutionary" task. Those who could teach would teach, those who could cook would cook. Participation would be "voluntary," but everyone was expected to participate. A work schedule would be set up, and each woman would be present in accordance with this schedule.

My wife, Norma, had been a teacher in Cuba, and therefore she was expected to teach at the *círculo*. She was, however, not interested in propagandizing children for the Revolution. She did not wish to work without pay, nor did she want to give up her time, including that spent with me on weekends.

Norma's reluctance to participate drew an angry response from

Navarro, who told her: "This is for the children. It must be done. In Cuba the women are making great sacrifices. They cannot go out, they cannot dress the way you can. They are working in the fields, and it is a privilege to live abroad. You must forget about going out."

Norma was accused of not being "ideologically strong," and she was told that I would be directed to concern myself more about her attitudes.

"Leyda," wife of "Julio," chief of the European section of D.G.I. in Havana, was also visiting Paris at this time, and she and López conferred with me about my wife's behavior. "If your wife cannot give you full attention and cannot go out with you, or take the children out in the sun, remember that it is for the good of the Revolution," Leyda asserted.

I objected to Navarro's treatment of my wife and said, "I don't even know who that woman is."

"She is a revolutionary. She has made sacrifices for the Revolution."

"Well," I replied, "I, too, am a revolutionary. I have fought for the Revolution and I know what I have done for the Revolution, but I don't know what she has done. She is probably an opportunist and wants to make the *círculo* another step in her career."

"You must not speak like that," Leyda cautioned. "That is not the way of a true revolutionary."

I angrily replied: "Look, don't give me lessons on revolutionary conduct. You put your daughters in a *círculo* in Cuba and they got lice, they had eye troubles and other sicknesses, they were under-nourished, and so you took them out. You should have discussed this with the director of the *círculo* instead of removing them. You had relatives with whom you could place the children during the day, but other revolutionaries didn't and they had to leave their children there."

The end result of the discussions was that the *círculo* would be established. Whereas it had been hoped the work would be "voluntary," it would now be clearly obligatory. One point won by us, however, was that a work schedule would not be imposed upon the wives. Rather, schedules for participation would be worked out by the women with a commission that was set up, composed of the D.G.I. chief, the second in command, and several other members of the staff.

69

Which is the drop that overflows the cup? The ill will aroused by Norma's rebellion lingered on, and she found herself ostracized from the social life of the Cubans in Paris. She was not invited to some functions, and when she was invited, she was shunned by other wives. She was criticized for dressing well—while the other women, less courageous, would buy five pairs of identical shoes, or three identical dresses, hoping that their husbands would not be aware of their unrevolutionary extravagances. I was faulted, too: I had five suits, when two or three were considered sufficient, and there were hints that I must be careful, for that smacked too much of the petit bourgeoisie. So did the fact that we liked to entertain a great deal at our home.

Then there was the matter of the salaries: the *Centro* staff was told that a policy of austerity was in effect in Cuba, and we must also participate. This participation was to take the form of giving back such portions of our salaries as we did not require for basic living. The staff was told that we must give up things: if we had wines with our dinner, we must dispense with them; if we ate desserts, we must forego them. As a small concession, the Ministry of Foreign Relations, which had been paying eighty percent of our rental costs in Paris, would now pay the full costs. I rebelled at relinquishing any substantial portion of my pay. I would be asked sarcastically, "Well, and what's wrong with you? " and I would answer, "I have heavy expenses."

And so at some point the cup spills over, and a decision is reached, and a person's life makes a dramatic and total turn. There had been occasions during the past months when Norma and I had brought up the possibility of leaving the *Centro*, and communism, and Cuba, but this had been oblique, half-joking talk. Serious talk, no, for such a move seemed almost too transcendental to think about. I never quite faced the possibility squarely. Norma had, in her own mind, but she was unsure about bringing up the matter with me except in offhanded ways. Families had broken up in Cuba over just such questions as this, ideological differences which had forced husbands and wives apart, brothers and sisters, children and parents.

Not acknowledgèd, nevertheless there, the decision began taking shape within my mind. Perhaps it had been made long before, and I had been shunting it aside, and then finally I could neither ignore nor evade it. There came a comparatively quiet day at the *Centro*, and I had time for my own thoughts. I faced myself and faced reality. examining alternatives and weighing consequences. There could as likely be unhappy consequences for failing to act, as for taking action. I had been at my Paris post almost two years now, and it was possible that I would soon be transferred back to Cuba. If I did return home, I might never have another good opportunity to make my break.

I knew not where it would lead, but that day I came to my decision.

That night, in bed, I spoke to my wife. I had not dared say anything earlier: I could not be sure there were no microphones hidden somewhere in the house. Using a sheet to muffle my voice, I said: "I have something to tell you. A decision I've made."

"But, why so low? " she asked. "You make me nervous."

"There may be a microphone here. They might hear us, and tomorrow we would be prisoners and on our way to Cuba. Look, I've decided to break with communism."

Norma alternated between joy and confusion. She hardly seemed to know what to say. We whispered back and forth.

It was a night without sleep. We talked until the early morning hours, considering how we could make our break, how we could get away, what we would do afterwards.

The time was the beginning of November. There would be many more sleepless nights and restless days in the weeks ahead.

When I had first arrived in Paris, I became acquainted with another *oficial* named Miguel Amantegui (code name "Antonio"), who, like myself, served as a third secretary. Amantegui had lived most of his youth in Paris and been educated there, and he spoke French fluently. Amantegui personally knew Piñeiro, the chief of D.G.I., and he had been picked for intelligence work in France because of his French upbringing. I early noticed a coolness toward Amantegui on the part of the *Centro* chief, although the reason for this attitude was not apparent. Then, one day, Amantegui was instructed to take a report to Moscow immediately. He left for that city, and did not return to Paris. Days passed, and the *oficiales* wondered where Amantegui was. López told his staff, "Amantegui has committed an error, and he has been sent to Cuba for a hearing." The nature of the "error" was not explained. Amantegui was not seen again, at least not in Paris.

Having decided to make my break, I remembered the Amantegui case and the lesson to be derived therefrom. I decided if ever I were ordered to go to Moscow or Prague I would defect immediately. I arranged a code with my wife: should I at any time phone her and say, "I have too much urgent work, and I can't take you the medicine you wanted," she would know that she was to gather the children and flee the apartment. I would go to the airport, as if departing for Moscow as instructed, but would then leave the airport and proceed to a prearranged spot to meet my family. I had no intention of becoming a second Amantegui.

I discussed with my wife possible ways in which we might defect. This was not simply a matter of walking out of the *Centro:* we would need outside assistance—assistance in hiding, in getting to another country, and, most important, in setting up new lives for ourselves. We carefully considered approaching the American Embassy in Paris, but finally discarded this idea as being potentially dangerous. The staff of the Cuban Embassy were constantly told that any Cubans who sought asylum with the Americans would be turned away: the Americans would suspect them of being infiltrators or provocateurs and would refuse to help. This might or might not be true, but if it did happen to us, we would be at the mercy of D.G.I. This was too great a risk to take.

We settled upon a plan to appeal to a Catholic organization. Both of us had been members of the Catholic Youth, and the Catholics were known to be active in helping people leave Cuba and assisting them to get started in new countries. It was a matter of selecting and making contact with the right organization or person.

Then I received a rude shock. López one day handed me the files on two men with whom Intelligence had made contact and who would be serving as *agentes.* Both men were Catholic priests, members of what they called "the revolutionary left of the Church." The priests were to be in the charge of myself and a D.G.I. collaborator, Luis Alberto Gutiérrez (code name "Reyes").

I immediately reconsidered my plan to contact Catholics in my effort to break away. If there were two priests working for Cuban Intelligence, there might be more—what if I were to appeal to one of these? The results would be disastrous for our family.

No further thought was given to approaching a Catholic organization. Instead, a new plan was formulated. There was a couple, W.

and A. A., now living in the United States who had been close friends of ours in Cuba. However, we had not been in touch with them for years. At the Paris apartment house, the mail was handled by the concierge, and since there were a number of Cubans living at 10 Rue Faraday, there was always the chance one of them might get a letter meant for someone else. And if it had become known that we were receiving mail from the United States, we would have fallen under grave suspicion.

Now, however, the risk would have to be taken. Norma wrote a letter to A. A. It was a normal, chatty letter, aimed only at reestablishing contact. It contained no hint of our intentions. As a precaution against an answering letter falling into the wrong hands, I requested the concierge to be careful to give my mail only to me personally, a request which I supported with a gift box of Cuban cigars.

And now began a period of nervous waiting, waiting which was to become all too familiar.

In this particular instance, however, the wait was not too long. A. A. replied within a few days, expressing delight at hearing from her old friend and giving details of their life in the States.

Norma now wrote a second, bolder letter, telling of her unhappiness and stating that "the brother of Panchito ought to be reunited with you." "Panchito"—nickname for Francisco—was one of Orlando's brothers; the Castros knew that the A's would understand that the oblique reference was to myself. As she wrote the letter, Norma cried. So much to say, so little that could be said, and the fate of our family in the balance. She asked the A's for suggestions as to what could be done.

Before mailing the letter, I made certain that I was not being followed. Even so, an additional precaution had been taken: the letter was written in such a way that anyone reading it might think it was of Norma's making alone, and that I had had nothing to do with it. In the event the letter should somehow fall into the hands of Cuban Intelligence, we hoped that I would be questioned about my "wife's" actions before any punitive measures were taken, and this might give us enough time to escape.

An ironic result of the ambiguous wording of the letter was that the A's, upon reading it, were themselves uncertain whether I was involved, or whether the letter represented Norma's feelings alone.

A second letter from A. A. arrived, and it directed that a telephone call be made to her brother, E., who also lived in the States. The phone number was included in the letter. At this time the Cuban *oficiales* in Paris were going through one of the periods of close surveillance by French Counter-Intelligence, and I decided not to make the call from our apartment or a public booth. Instead, I waited two days until there was a quiet time at the Embassy, with few people about, and then placed the call from there. I knew the call would not be listed on the phone bill for two months or so, and by that time I would, hopefully, be well gone. Even so, I gave the operator the name "Armando," which was that of a Cuban army officer who was visiting Paris and who was considered to be a somewhat careless individual.

The conversation with E. was a cautious one. E. wanted to assure himself that he was indeed speaking with me. He asked me questions about my childhood, and when these were answered satisfactorily, E. was convinced. He said: "O.K. Now, you want to come to the United States—is that right? "

I replied affirmatively.

E. asked why I simply did not go to the American Embassy and ask asylum. I explained my fears about this.

There was momentary silence at the other end, while E. seemed to do some thinking, and then he said: "Look, perhaps there is an answer. My uncle and aunt are traveling to Europe in a few weeks. They will be in Paris, and then I think they are going on to Luxembourg."

We talked further, and I emphasized the need for caution. E. assured me that the aunt and uncle could be trusted completely.

And now, still more days of waiting. Anguished waiting, uncertainty, fear, the passage of time versus the steadfastness of our courage. We would go walking along the paths of the Bois de Boulogne. This was the only place we could be sure we weren't being overheard, and the quiet strolls in idyllic surroundings served to soothe and clear our troubled spirits. They days wore on, and Norma became increasingly uneasy; she worried that D.G.I. would kidnap one of our children in order to maintain control over us. I reassured her, but I, too, was deeply concerned. Where was all this taking us. Always there were questions, speculation, more questions: How would contact be made? Had D.G.I. intercepted any of the letters?

What if we heard nothing further—what would we do then? I had arranged a signal with my wife to be used should I suddenly be ordered to Moscow. Now we arranged a second signal: if contact were made with either of us while we were apart, that person would call the other and say certain medicines were needed. There would be nothing unusual about such a request, particularly at the time, since both of our children were feeling poorly.

Twenty days went by, a small eternity, and finally one afternoon, while at work at the chancellery, I received a call from Norma. Barely containing her excitement, she asked me to bring home nose drops for little Osvaldo. I shot out of the chancellery and, driving an Embassy Peugeot, made the trip to my home, which ordinarily took about fifteen minutes, in half that time.

I entered our apartment, greeted Norma, and quickly looked around. I expected to see a visitor, and when I saw no one, I thought perhaps the visitor was hiding in order to give me a surprise.

"No," said Norma, "no, there is no one here. There was a man, but he left. He said he was E's uncle."

"What else did he say? " I asked anxiously. "Are you sure he was the uncle? "

"Well, he told about E. and his family, and about A. A., and he spoke Spanish. He said not to be frightened—that everything would be all right." The visitor had spent half an hour with Norma, asking questions and talking with her. He had preferred that she not call me until he had left, saying that he did not feel it wise that we should meet in the apartment. He had asked that I meet him the following evening at 7 at a café called Le Franc Tiräilleur. He told Norma he would recognize me because he had a photograph of me, but in addition I was to carry a brightly-wrapped box in which the man had brought candy for our children.

I had strong misgivings. This was not going the way I had visualized it. Amateurs playing at espionage were not to my liking. This matter was too serious, too dangerous. I could not even be sure as to whom I was dealing with. True, in order to identify himself, the man had brought a letter from A. A., as well as one of the letters Norma had written. The letter from A. A. stated that the bearer was a "friend" who could be trusted. I knew, however, that in intelligence work it is easy to forge signatures. As for Norma's letter, it was not inconceivable that it might have been intercepted at some point. If

Cuban Intelligence had become aware of my intentions, they might well have provided an agent—perhaps a Soviet agent—with the proper papers and had him call on us, posing as a friend.

I questioned Norma closely: what had the man looked like, how had he acted, what had he said? I examined every detail, and I made my wife go over and over the visitor's statements. I searched for any clue that might indicate the man was an enemy and not a friend. This whole affair was increasingly dangerous, and I was determined to be as careful as possible. That was another sleepless night for us.

The following day was a routine one at the chancellery, where I was on duty. My tasks were to take care of the diplomatic pouch, as well as deal with matters of protocol. I was edgy, and every time another *oficial* spoke to me, I searched the man's face and his words, wondering whether behind the façade of normality there was suspicion. And every time I saw other officials speaking among themselves, I felt they were saying: "We're going to catch this guy when he goes to the meeting, we'll catch him with his hands in the jar."

I lunched by myself at a nearby cafeteria, and early in the afternoon I told my chief that I was going out, explaining that I planned to look over possible future rendezvous points. Using a Volkswagen that belonged to the *Centro,* I drove around Paris for several hours, making certain that I was not being followed, and then I headed toward Le Franc Tirailleur.

I parked three blocks from the café, got out of the car, looked around, and began walking. Under my arm was the candy box. Under my coat was a Browning pistol, a gift from López when I had arrived in Paris. If this were a trap, I was prepared to shoot my way out.

I walked slowly. The month was February. The weather was cold, and I wore a topcoat. It was already dark, but street lights provided good illumination, and I could keep my eye on passersby. I felt confident that no one was following me. I had parked on a street which ran in front of the café, and I could clearly see its lights as I walked toward it. The café was typical of its kind, partly indoors, partly outdoors, so that either portion could be used, depending on the weather. Now only a few customers sat on the outside terrace.

I did not get to enter the café. A man came from the opposite direction, his approach timed so that he encountered me just as I reached the café. The man wore an overcoat, no hat, and was of medium height. He asked, "Are you Castro?"

76

"Yes—yes, I am Castro."

"Well," said the man, breaking into a smile. "I am the uncle of E. and A. A." He placed his arm on my shoulder in a gesture of friendship. "We have much to talk about."

I touched my pistol, and the man noticed the action. He asked, "What is that? "

I replied, "Something because I have no confidence in this."

"You can have confidence, you must believe me," the man said earnestly. He stopped under a street light and showed the letter of introduction from A. A. I carefully perused the note. It could be genuine, but then again, it might be a forgery. There could be no assurance as to its authenticity.

I came to a decision, a showdown born of uncertainty, an end to pretense. I said bluntly: "Look, I do not trust you, but it does not matter. I have taken a step, and I am determined to go through with it, and when I came to this meeting I was ready for whatever might happen. If you are an enemy, you can try to do whatever you wish, and I am prepared for anything, anything at all that I have to do."

"There is no need to talk that way," the man said reassuringly. "Do not be afraid. I will help you."

The meeting lasted a brief ten minutes. Another was set for the following day. I stated frankly that I still had no confidence, and intended to do some checking.

The next day I went to a telephone exchange and from there made an overseas call to E. I told E. of the contact that had been made and asked him to describe his uncle. The description E. provided fitted the man who had met me. When E. mentioned the letter of introduction from A. A. which his uncle carried, I was convinced of the uncle's authenticity.

That evening I again saw the uncle—he brought his wife along this time—and this was a friendlier meeting. Again we were at a café, and we spent hours discussing ways by which I could make my break and our family flee from France. Safety was the prime consideration, and this could best be achieved if all of us were quietly and swiftly spirited out of the country. Should Norma and the children leave first, and I follow? Was it preferable to get out of Paris by plane? Train? Car? A minimum of fuss was desirable because this would lessen the chances of the escape being detected before it could be completed.

The uncle and aunt, after spending several weeks in Paris, intended to go on to Luxembourg. A feasible plan seemed to be for us to accompany them. An added attraction of the idea was that there was no D.G.I. *Centro* in Luxembourg.

That night I told Norma of the plan that was being formulated. She liked it and hoped that it could be undertaken without much delay.

I met the uncle several more times at different cafés in order to work out details of the projected departure. Getting to Luxembourg was not in itself a full solution. Eventually I could be traced there. I would need some sort of protection. Very much in my mind were the recent attempts by Communist agents to kidnap a Chinese defector in the Hague and a Cuban defector in Mexico.

The uncle said, "When you arrive in Luxembourg, you will have to ask the Americans for help."

"But will they give it? " I asked. "Won't they think I am a plant by Cuban Intelligence? "

"You will have to take the chance. You will have to convince them you are genuinely seeking asylum."

And from this conversation a new facet of the plan evolved. If I could prove that I was truly a defector—yes, there might be a way I could prove this to the satisfaction of the Americans. If I could bring with me the *Centro*'s secret documents, the Americans would surely accept that I was a legitimate defector, and not a plant. It would be a difficult task to get those documents, however—not only were they contained in locked boxes within a safe, they were also protected by an alarm system.

Those were taut days. Norma was exceedingly apprehensive. Every time there was a knock on the door, she was fearful that someone had come to inform her that her husband was under arrest and the family was being sent back to Cuba. On one occasion López had made a casual visit, while I was away, and she later reported that López had looked at her "strangely," as if aware of something. When I would arrive home from work, Norma would complain about her constant worry and would bombard me with questions: Is there anything new? Do you think anyone is suspicious? The waiting was not doing much for my nerves, either.

Over a period of weeks I removed, a few items at a time, most of the family's clothes and personal possessions from the apartment.

When the break was finally made, we would have no need to carry anything. We could walk out, and if anyone was watching, there would be no cause for suspicion.

I was scheduled for Sunday duty at the *Centro* on March 31. It was less likely there would be other *oficiales* about on that day. This would provide the best opportunity for making a try for the documents. If anyone else should be there, I could stay at the *Centro* as late as necessary, making a pretense of working. Then once the other person or persons had left, I would make my move.

Nildo Alvarez, the D.G.I. collaborator, was returning to Cuba with his family that Sunday. A farewell party was planned, and Norma agreed to provide a typical Cuban dish. Saturday evening was a busy one, the Alvarezes getting ready for their trip, visitors coming and going, preparations being made for the party.

We were up until late, and even when we finally went to bed we did not fall asleep until shortly before dawn. Upon awakening later, I found a gray day, gloomy and rainy, the temperature near freezing.

X

Escape

NORMA ATTENDED THE FAREWELL PARTY FOR NILDO Alvarez and his wife, who were leaving for Havana that evening. Cubans love to make a big thing out of departures, and, traditionally, close relatives, distant relatives, friends, and even acquaintances will go to the airport to see the person off. The people at this farewell party were planning to do the same, and Norma was expected to come along. She demurred, explaining that she was to meet her French teacher and the teacher's wife, and she had no way of reaching them to cancel the engagement. Nildo expressed hurt; Norma acted as lighthearted as she could manage, trying hard to hide her uneasiness, and apparently succeeding, because no suspicions were aroused.

After the party and the emotional farewells, and the "We'll-see-you-in-Cubas," Norma returned to our apartment. She prepared herself and the two boys for the long journey ahead, and late in the afternoon they set out. It was cold and raining, and the concierge commented on the weather, wondering why they chose to go out at this time.

Norma replied, "We're meeting my husband," and immediately realized the inadequacy of the answer, since the man might well ask why her husband didn't drive by and pick them up in a car. But the concierge smiled and said nothing further, and now they were outside in the cold drizzle.

They walked several blocks and came to a predesignated spot where the uncle and aunt waited. Norma had suffered further uneasiness—what if the couple failed to keep the appointment? —but they were there and greeted them and took them in hand. The boys were helped into a parked car, and Norma followed, but there was a momentary difficulty with one-and-a-half-year-old Osvaldo's stroller. The stroller did not fit into the car, nor into the trunk compartment.

The uncle said: "Well, what for? They are leaving so much behind, they might as well leave this, too."

The stroller was left on the sidewalk. Only Orlando, Jr., three and a half years old, objected, complaining, "Mama, what are they doing with Osvaldito's *coche*—why are they throwing it away? " His mother reassured him.

Norma and the children were driven to an apartment building and taken into an apartment which the uncle had rented for this purpose. Here the personal belongings they would take with them had been stored.

Now they would wait . . .

My guard duty at the Embassy was to begin at one in the afternoon, and I arrived promptly. The code official was waiting to leave, and he did so immediately upon my arrival. The code man was accompanied by several other members of the staff, all going out for a Sunday afternoon on the town. Still in the residence were the ambassador's wife, Doris, and her four daughters. Yraida, a servant who helped the cook and did miscellaneous tasks, was also there, as was a Cuban army captain known as *El Francés,* who had been visiting Paris.

I settled down to relax as best I could. I picked a comfortable chair in the small sitting room of the code official's apartment within the apartment. For reading I chose—was this Freudian? —case books prepared by G-2 detailing their operations against spies and counterrevolutionaries.

There would be long, nervous hours ahead. I dared not make my move until I knew that my family had reached safety. I had arranged with Norma that as soon as she arrived at the secret apartment, she was to phone me at the Embassy and say: "We've arrived at the teacher's house. We'll wait for you to join us for dinner. We are all right."

The party for Nildo and his wife had been the big hitch. Norma could not avoid going to it without causing suspicion, and since she had to attend, I had to wait until it was over and my family were able to make their break.

I did decide to make a trial run. I waited until two-thirty in order to be sure that all was tranquil at the Embassy, that no one was keeping a suspicious eye on me. Putting down my book, I strolled the thirty yards to the door of the *Centro*. The door had two locks, and I had keys to both of these. I unlocked the door and entered a small space, upon which two additional doors faced, one leading into the *Centro*'s office, the other into a room containing the safe utilized by the Intelligence staff. One wall of the small space was made of cardboard, the nail heads clearly visible. Actually, one of these nails was part of an ingenious alarm system: unless the nail was removed—and it was indistinguishable from the others—an alarm would sound if the doors to either the office or the room with the safe were opened. Because the Intelligence *oficiales* individually had occasion to use these quarters on Sundays and in the evenings, when no one else might be about, all knew how to disconnect the alarm. The chief and the second in command alone knew, however, how the alarm worked or where it sounded.

I removed the nail and placed it on the floor in a corner. The code official kept a ring of keys, but on his days off he turned these over to the guard officer, and I now had them. Two of these keys opened two locks on the door to the room with the safe. I entered the room and went to the safe. On the face of the safe door was a metal cover, which I swung to one side, revealing five combination locks in a circle. A large, special key, which was also kept on the code official's key ring, had to be inserted in each of these locks and turned in accordance with the lock's combination. The combinations were different for each lock, and each official had had to memorize all five of the combinations. If the combinations were properly worked, when the same key was inserted and turned in a central keyhole, the door could be opened. I worked the combinations, heard the resulting clicks, and then put the key into the keyhole. There was another click, louder than the others, and I was able to swing the door open.

Within the large safe were metal boxes in which each of the Intelligence officials kept his papers. In a separate, locked compartment inside the safe were the boxes used by López, the chief, and Díaz, the second in command. In a lapse in security, the key to this inner compartment was included among those on the master key ring. I tried several keys, found the proper one, and opened the compartment. There stood two boxes, one red, one gray.

Testing a key which had been fashioned for this purpose by a locksmith who had used my own key as a model, I unlocked the gray box, which belonged to the second in command. This was but a trial run; I did not take any documents, nor did I touch the red box of the chief. This box was different than the others, and I had no key for it.

Removing a mass of documents from the Embassy would be a problem, I had foreseen. The previous day, therefore, I had placed a red valise near the safe. Because this room was used as an occasional storeroom, nobody had taken note of the bag.

I put everything back as it had been. The plan might work well when the time came, but I knew that the danger would be great. To open the door to the room, open the safe, open the inner compartment, load the documents in the valise, close everything again—this would take three to five minutes, and if someone should enter at any moment after I had opened the inner compartment, I would be caught with no possible explanation that anyone would accept.

One other security lapse worked slightly in my favor. López, the chief, had to ring the outside doorbell like anyone else before he could enter the Embassy. He had no key of his own. The sound of the bell ringing would give me a few moments' warning, although this might not be sufficient.

Uneasy though I was, I was determined to proceed with my plan. I had one bit of "insurance." When I had dressed to come to work, I had placed my pistol, fully loaded, under my shirt. If I had to use the weapon in order to escape, I was prepared to.do so.

As I was shutting the safe, I thought I heard the doorbell. Was this the first ring? Or had the bell been ringing—perhaps the servant was already opening the door.

I hurried out of the room, closed the door, closed the outer door, and returned to the chair where I had been reading.

Yraida opened the door to the Embassy, and López entered,

accompanied by Pedro Machado (code name "Saul"), an Intelligence officer who doubled as the local head of Prensa Latina, the Cuban news wire service. I forced myself to appear relaxed, hoping that my throbbing heart was not as apparent outwardly as it was inwardly.

The two men greeted me casually, and López asked for the key ring. With this in hand, they headed toward the *Centro*'s quarters. Both were dressed in laborers' clothing. The African country of Guinea had broken diplomatic relations with France, and having withdrawn its Embassy, it had given to the Cuban government the building which had formerly been occupied by the Guinean Embassy. To this edifice the Cuban chancellery was to be transferred, but before the move could be accomplished, extensive alterations and fixing-up were required. In order to carry this out, all members of the Cuban staff were expected to give up one of their days off each week and do "voluntary" work at the building. On this Sunday López and Machado had been doing their stint.

The two men remained in the *Centro*'s quarters. I strained to hear what they were saying, but was unable to do so. Was their visit purely coincidental—or were they checking on me? Through my mind raced recent events as I tried to remember whether I had done or said anything which might have aroused suspicions. Would they find anything amiss? I had heard—the *oficiales* were sometimes told—that little traps had been set about the office, that objects in the safe were placed in certain ways, and if anything was disturbed, this would be apparent to the chiefs.

To keep my weapon well concealed, I had not removed my coat all the time I was in the Embassy, despite the warmth generated by a heating system. Now I sat tensely, one hand under my jacket and near the butt of the gun. I continued reading—or more accurately, made a pretense of reading—my book.

Fifteen minutes later the men emerged from the *Centro*. I did not look up. The floor was wooden, and I could tell by their footsteps that they were heading toward me. I braced myself, ready to leap up and level my weapon.

"How come the alarm is disconnected? " López asked. I silently exclaimed—damn! In my hurry to get out of the room with the safe I had forgotten to put the alarm nail back in place. But I saw that López did not appear to be suspicious, merely curious.

"I took this book out," I replied, indicating the volume I was

84

holding, "and since I was going to return it in a few minutes, I didn't bother to set it again." López was satisfied. He returned the key ring and told me that he and Machado were off to attend the Alvarez's farewell party, and would afterward go to the airport to say goodbye.

I tried to relax into my chair. I attempted to read; the words meant nothing to me.

A bell rang again, startling me, sending a new flood of cold fears coursing through me. It was the bell to the rear door, a door which opened from the kitchen onto Pergolais Street. Ordinarily this door was used only by servants and deliverymen on weekdays. This added to my uncertainty: Who would be at the door on a Sunday?

The bell kept ringing, and no one seemed about to answer it, and so I walked to the kitchen and opened it myself, my hand halfway toward my gun. I found Jorge Solis (code name "Roberto") waiting outside. Solis was a fellow *oficial* at the Center. We greeted, and Solis explained, "I have to make a contact, and I left the address in the office." I gave him the key ring, and Solis went to the *Centro*. He was there a few minutes, then returned the keys and left.

Nevertheless, I was wary. Solis had seemed to be somewhat agitated—was he late for his appointment? Or had López spotted an indication of something amiss and sent Solis to check on me? I recalled my discussions with López over Norma's refusal to participate in the study circle. I thought back over my work—or lack of work—the past weeks. I had, in truth, not been doing a good job with my contacts and agents: I had deliberately missed meetings, later reporting that my contacts had not shown up, or that there had been suspicious movements at the rendezvous points. I had had no interest in my work; I had been gradually withdrawing from my responsibilities. Nor had I wanted to draw any more people into the Cuban Intelligence network.

Had López become aware of all this, and did he now suspect, perhaps, what I was prepareing to do? I forced myself not to panic, fought down a compelling urge to flee. On no account could I do that—even if I dropped the plan to seize the documents, I dared not leave until I knew that my family were in safety.

A bell rang again—the front doorbell. I thought grimly, "Something is going to blow up here." This time it was a new *oficial*, one who had recently arrived in Paris. Being new to the city, he had no friends to spend Sunday with and so had decided to utilize the time studying the *Centro*'s files. He explained to me that he intended to learn more about the *situación operativa* in Paris, as well as about his own contacts and the cases in which he was involved. He planned to remain in the *Centro* throughout the afternoon, and I knew this would prevent me from removing the documents, unless I used force, which would be so risky I did not want to do it except as a last resort.

"Look," I suggested, "why don't you use today to study the Paris metros? The metros will be important in your work, and at the same time you can also learn more about the city. You must know Paris and you must know how to get around. Better you do that than to study files at this point." I chatted with the new official for fifteen minutes and convinced him that he ought to go out and look at Paris. "Here, take these tickets to the metro"—I had several in my pocket—"and use them to travel around." I indicated interesting areas for "study," and the *oficial* happily set out on his trip of exploration.

Shortly before five o'clock, Doris Castellanos, the ambassador's wife, came and asked if I would like a lemonade, for she was preparing some. "Yes," I replied, "thank you." She returned with the drink, and we talked for a while about our respective children.

Doris sensed my unease. "What's the matter? Don't you feel well? "

I grinned, striving for casualness. I told her: "Perhaps this isn't my day. I'm a bit under the weather, been thinking about my problems."

"So young and always gay, and you have problems? " She laughed, and a little later returned to the ambassadorial quarters.

Still no word from Norma. I mentally braced myself: control, self-discipline, everything depended on my self-discipline, nothing is wrong, be patient. Word will come. And yet, if . . . I had to kill time, and so set out for a stroll through the Embassy. I chatted with one of the ambassador's daughters, then had a few words with the visiting captain.

A new problem loomed: I had planned to leave the Embassy through the kitchen door at the rear. I had parked my Volkswagen on the street near the door so that I could get away rapidly. But Yraida, the servant, had been napping and now she had awakened and begun working in the kitchen. To make my exit, I would have to walk by her, and I would be carrying my valise. She might very well become suspicious, knowing that I was supposed to be on guard duty.

At six-thirty the telephone rang. I answered, and it was Norma. Speaking in a low voice, she said: "We just arrived at the teacher's house. We are going to eat here, but we'll wait for you." She added reassuringly: "We are fine, perfect. The children are fine." There was a sharp note of excitement in her voice, carefully controlled.

"Very good," I said. "I'll see you soon."

I immediately hung up the phone. In a not-running run I went to the window of the large ballroom, and from here I scanned Foch Avenue below. For at that moment I had severe doubts, felt almost sure that the others suspected something was wrong. I looked out to see if there were any Embassy vehicles about, perhaps someone waiting below or entering the building. There was no sign of anything— even so, I felt little reassurance.

I now virtually repeated my previous operation. One difference was the matter of my own key. Each *oficial* kept his box in the safe, and there was a separate key for each box. The *oficial* did not retain his key on his person, however, but instead left it with the code official, who kept all the keys in a small drawer under the Teletype machine. During my trial run, I had not bothered with my own box and key, but now I retrieved my key from the drawer and headed toward the *Centro*.

I reopened the doors—no need to disconnect the alarm this time: it had not yet been reconnected. In the safe room, I used the special key, worked the combinations, and unlocked the safe. I took the red valise and placed it, open, on the floor in front of the safe. A moment's hesitation, and then I quickly opened the little door to the inner compartment.

I was now committed. This was the real thing and there was no turning back—the moment of truth, and all I could do now was to continue with the operation, and do this with all possible dispatch. I was nervous; my hands shook; I was clumsy; and visually, frighteningly real in my mind were the terrible consequences should I be caught. I considered dropping everything and fleeing, running, escaping, but somehow I continued at my task, functioning almost mechanically despite my deadening fear.

The chief's red box was heavy, made of an alloy, rectangular, about a foot and a half long and six inches wide. I made no attempt to open this. I dumped the whole box into the valise. I opened the gray, metal box belonging to the second in command. Watching the *segundo* taking papers from, or placing them in, a red, plastic briefcase, I had gathered that these were Díaz's more important documents. The briefcase now lay on top of a batch of papers inside the box. I grabbed it and dropped in into the valise. I took a fistful of papers, too nervous to spend any time being selective, and these also went into the valise. I opened my own box; everything in it went into the valise.

There were the boxes of the other officials, but time was fleeting. Every second increased the danger, and with the papers of the chief and the *segundo,* I knew that I had secured the most important documents in the *Centro.*

I closed the safe, locked it, and pocketed the key after removing it from the ring. I twirled the combination a number of times. With the key missing, it would be a while before anyone could get the safe open.

I picked up my valise and started out, not stopping to set the alarm. In the hallway I paused to see if I could hear anything. All was quiet. I took my overcoat but did not put it on. I wanted to be able to reach my gun rapidly, if I had to.

I carried the valise in my left hand, my overcoat draped over it, not quite concealing it. I would now have to traverse a goodly portion of the Embassy to get to the kitchen and the exit. My senses acutely alert to any sign of danger, I walked rapidly, and as silently as I could, almost on my toes.

Yraida was in the kitchen and immediately noticed the valise and overcoat. "Where . . . ," she began, "say, are you going to Cuba? " If she wondered about my guard duty, she said nothing.

"Yes," I said, "I'm going. Would you like me to deliver any messages? "

"Well, say hello to my family there, will you? "

"Sure. *Hasta luego.*"

"*Que le vaya bien.*"

Out the door. To the car. Cold rain; cold fear. A curse—where were the keys to the car? Fumbling, fumbling in the wet and chill and fright, until the keys were located in a pocket of the overcoat.

I drove toward the house where my family waited. I drove swiftly, disregarding safety, hardly conscious of what I was doing. The first cautious relief was creeping in.

My wife greeted me with tears, and we embraced, the harrowing wait, the long and fearful days now over.

Then, the final lap—the family bundled into a car, a fast drive through the night to neighboring Luxembourg. Here I asked the American Embassy for political asylum in the United States, and this was granted.

The nightmare had ended.

Epilogue

WE NOW LIVE IN THE UNITED STATES. I AM STUDYING English, and I plan to begin a career in a field totally unrelated to my previous occupation. We are safely and comfortably esconced in suburbia and have adjusted well to our new environment.

The people around us do not know who we are. My identity must remain secret. I cannot fly in commercial planes, because planes are hijacked, and in Cuba I might be recognized—in which case my existence would terminate most abruptly.

My children will grow up Americanized, and perhaps they will be American citizens.

I am educating myself about my new country. I read avidly, watch television, go to movies. On one occasion I had the opportunity to go to Washington, and I went to the Lincoln Memorial. Although my understanding of the English language was not yet altogether adequate, I read each word of the Gettysburg Address inscribed there. My reaction was, *"Formidable!"* How well Lincoln knew and expressed the conflicts that are fought in the minds of men! From the back of the Memorial I could see the distant site of President Kennedy's grave. Years ago—an age ago—I had battled the troops Kennedy had sent to the Bay of Pigs. Afterwards, I visited the darkened room where Lincoln died, and Ford's Theatre across the street, with its Lincoln museum. Again, I was fascinated by the historic momentos of American tradition.

In the history of our own age, I have played a certain role. In choosing freedom, I hope I have contributed to freedom through my example. My private hope is that some day my actions will help my country regain its own freedom.

On the scoreboard of the Cold War, I chalked up my share of points. Through the information and documents I provided, I was able to:

Identify more than 150 agents and contacts of Cuban Intelligence.

Reveal the extent to which Intelligence has taken over the Cuban diplomatic service, as well as other governmental organizations.

Reveal the functioning of D.G.I. in Cuba and its operations abroad.

Disclose what happened to Dominican leader Francisco Caamaño following his mysterious disappearance.

Disclose the full magnitude of the Castro-Guervara subversive plan for South America.

Reveal the secret agreement between Fidel Castro and Moscow which today is virtually converting Cuba into a Soviet colony.

In the field of espionage—the Gray World—I will not soon be forgotten, by East or West.

Appendix

A Brief History of D.G.I.

In the preceding chapters I have told the story of my career
with the Dirección General de Inteligencia. The espionage
system built up by the government of Cuba, with guidance and
assistance from the Soviet Union, has become one of the most
sophisticated in the world. Little has ever been written about
the D.G.I. The following, therefore, is an account of some of
its operations and personnel.

Fidel Castro's intelligence service had its genesis in the mountains of
eastern Cuba. The rebel movement, in 1957 and 1958, was engaged
in guerrilla warfare against the forces of Dictator Fulgencio Batista.
Campensinos—peasants—moved back and forth between the government and rebel zones, and some of these rural folk kept the guerrillas posted on the movements of the government's troops. In the
nearby city of Santiago and extending across the island there was a
clandestine rebel apparatus that served as a support organization for
the guerrillas, funneling funds, recruits, and supplies into the hills.
The underground also waged urban warfare—terrorism, sabotage,
propaganda—and this attrition eventually so weakened the regime
that the guerrilla forces were able to come down out of the hills and
take over the country and the government.

A major coup—from the viewpoint of attracting worldwide publicity to the rebel cause—was scored by the rebel intelligence service in 1958. The United States government, in an effort to maintain its neutrality in the Cuban civil war, suspended the shipment of weapons to the Batista regime in March 1958.

Nevertheless, the United States did subsequently provide Batista with live ammunition to replace practice warheads which had been previously sent to him by mistake under a mutual security agreement. What happened next has been described by Raúl Castro in an article he wrote titled "Operation Antiaircraft." Raúl recounted:

At the end of May, our Department of Rebel Intelligence handed me a photograph and a document of exceptional importance. It was a photograph taken inside the United States Naval Base at Guantánamo, where two of Batista's planes could be seen alongside a parked American truck loaded with ammunition. The insignia on the planes, alongside the U.S. emblem on a hut close to the airstrip, left no doubt as to those planes being Batista's and receiving help from the U.S. Naval Base at Guantánamo Bay. The other document, even more important, had been torn from a record book of war material dispatched from the Guantánamo Naval Base. Taken from the files of the base, it was dated May 8, 1958 and bore the signature of an authority in charge of such procedures. This was a detailed account of the shipment of North American war material by the U.S. Naval Base at Guantánamo to the Batista government.

Raúl Castro decided to utilize the opportunity thus presented in order to create an international furor. At this time the guerrillas were being severely harassed by Batista's air force, and Raúl felt that if he were to seize Americans living within the rebel zone and hold them, Batista would call off the air raids out of fear of injuring the captives. The rebels would use, Raúl decided, the shipment of ammunition to Batista as the pretext for the mass kidnapping.

With the victory of the rebel cause and the establishment of the Castro government, Castro set his sights on a larger target, the Caribbean and then the entire Southern Hemisphere. The first attempts at subversion were crude. Filibustering expeditions were dispatched to a number of countries, but were quickly wrapped up by the defense forces of these countries. Cuba turned to more sophisticated methods of subversion, and its intelligence operations were concerned mainly with supporting these efforts. The primary function of Cuban intelligence was, and has remained through the years, the support of subversion and guerrilla warfare in target countries, countries which have ranged geographically from Canada to Argentina, from the United States to Zanzibar. Cuban intelligence operations and subversive projects have usually been so interwoven that they have been virtually indistinguishable.

Cuban intelligence functions were originally the responsibility of G-2, a department of the Ministry of Interior. (Subsequently this section was named the *Departamento de Seguridad del Estado,* although it is still popularly known as "G-2.") In late 1961, owing to Cuba's increasing interest in foreign affairs, the *Dirección General de Inteligencia* (General Directorate of Intelligence) was created as a separate entity within the Interior Ministry. The D.G.I. is headed by Major Manuel Piñeiro Losada, who is First Vice-Minister and Technical Vice-Minister of the Ministry, the latter capacity giving him authority over D.G.I. Piñeiro's high rank attests to the importance attached by Castro to his espionage service. Piñeiro had been one of the guerrilla officers serving under Raúl Castro during the Revolution. At one time a student at Columbia University in New York, Piñeiro evidently met there the American girl who was to become his wife. Sporting a red beard, Piñeiro is sometimes known as *Barba Roja,* which, when one thinks about it, seems quite appropriate for the chief of Fidel Castro's Communist spy service.

One of the first functions of D.G.I. was the running of special schools for the training of Latin Americans in guerrilla warfare and subversive techniques. At one time, early in the sixties, as many as 1,500 men a year were being brought to Cuba for training. Once a major air and sea hub for travel in the hemisphere, Cuba's virtual exclusion from the hemispheric political system sharply cut down transportation means to and from the island. Nevertheless, flights have continued between Havana and Mexico City and Madrid, and there are also flights to and from Iron Curtain cities via Algeria. These circuitous routes were utilized to bring Latin Americans to Cuba, and use was also made of clandestine methods: Communist freighters and Cuban fishing boats.

Once in Havana, the trainees were grouped by nationality. Usually there were fifteen to twenty-five men in each group, although there might be as few as three. The various nationalities were gener-

94

ally kept apart, for security reasons as well as because the courses given to the different groups varied. Venezuelans concentrated on guerrilla operations and sabotage techniques. Chileans, coming from a country with a strong Communist Party, were coached on furthering the Communist cause through political methods. In special cases, emphasis was placed on techniques of agitation and propaganda in particular fields in which the trainees were involved in their homelands: unions, universities, intellectual organizations, or such.

Guerrilla warfare courses lasted three to six months, but occasionally as long as a year. Trainees showing particular promise were sometimes given additional training to become intelligence agents when they returned to their home countries. Appearing before an investigating committee of the Organization of American States in June 1967, a Venezuelan, Manuel Celestino Marcano Carrasquel, detailed the subversive preparation he had received in Cuba. Marcano testified:

I took courses in guerrilla and counter-guerrilla tactics, theory and practice; assembling and disassembling short and long weapons, automatic and semi-automatic weapons, especially some of the ones that were easiest to acquire, especially "Springfield," "Garand," "Fals," M-1, "Mendoza" machine guns, as well as the Mexican, the .30 and .50 caliber; theory and practice of firing long and short weapons; security measures; then rapid firing, which they call "Mexican defense." In explosives I was given a course that covered homemade bombs using chlorate, grenades, booby traps, "Molotov cocktails" of various kinds—including wickless, detonating wicks, blasting caps, calculation of charge. They put a great deal of emphasis on blowing up oil pipelines. . . . Then in topography: I took a course in map-making and map-reading, including reading of tactical maps, contour lines, intersection, reception, scientific orientation and practice with the compass.

There were a relatively large number of people in Marcano's original group, but most were eventually weeded out. He reported: "We began with 150 persons. After three months we numbered 50. Later the number was ten. Apparently they [the instructors] made a series of observations with regard to the ability and ductility of each individual."

The group was also given instruction in a range of intelligence and clandestine fields. This included: "Checks and counterchecks . . . Hiding places for making indirect contacts; places where it would have been possible to leave explosives, arms, money; the international post boxes for indirect correspondence on the basis of cryptography . . . Underground organization and structure at various levels. Photography . . . Infiltration . . . The falsification of documents, make-up, tailoring, simulation of dialects, phonetics, etc. This with regard to [false] identity."

Never before had so ambitious a program of subversion been launched by a small country. North Viet Nam has tried to subvert South Viet Nam; Cuba was aiming at subverting an entire continent. The Castro-Guevara program was one of the most systematized subversive schemes in the annals of the Cold War. The tentacles reached out from Havana to every corner of the continent.

Despite its ostracism by the Latin American community because of its continued efforts at subversion, the Castro regime has persisted in its program. What could only be termed an international conference to foment subversion was held in Havana from January 3 to 15, 1966. It was officially called the "First Conference of Solidarity of the Peoples of Africa, Asia, and Latin America," but for brevity's sake it has come to be known as the "Tricontinental Conference." The hosts were the Communist Party and government of Cuba, and the joint sponsors were the Communist-dominated Afro-Asian Peoples' Solidarity Organization, with headquarters in Cairo, and Latin American Communist parties and subversive groups. Attending were approximately 512 delegates, 64 observers, and 77 invited guests. The official delegates represented 82 countries and territories. The Soviet delegation, consisting of forty members, was the largest at the conference.

Whatever fiction may have existed that international communism did not engage in subversive practices was dispelled at the Tricontinental. The agenda was crowded with such phrases as "Struggle against imperialism . . . Struggle for complete national liberation . . . Intensification of all forms of struggle . . . Ways and means of aiding the liberation movements in Africa, Asia, and Latin America . . . Burning issues of the struggle . . . Anti-imperialist solidarity, and so on. In spite of splits within the conference, especially the Sino-Soviet division, the Tricontinental passed 73 resolutions on a variety of subjects. These were summed up in the declaration, "The Conference proclaims the inalienable right of the peoples to total political independence and to resort to all forms of struggle that are necessary, including armed struggle, in order to conquer that right." In a closing speech to the delegates, Fidel Castro declared that the Tricontinental had been "a great victory of the revolutionary movement."

Two permanent organizations grew out of the conference. The first, created by resolution of the conference itself, was the Organization of Solidarity of the Peoples of Africa, Asia, and Latin America, whose task was "to unite, coordinate, and further the struggle" on those three continents. The second organization was created by the 27 Latin American delegations after the close of the Tricontinental. On January 16 they announced establishment of the Latin American Organization of Solidarity (*Organización Latino-americana de Solidaridad*—O.L.A.S.). Its aim was "to utilize all the means within its reach in order to support the movements of liberation."

The O.L.A.S. was of especial interest to Castro and his regime. Through its establishment, a façade of international recognition and respectability—at least among the Communists—was granted to the subversive efforts directed by Cuba against other Latin American countries. The headquarters of O.L.A.S. was set up in Havana, and the First Conference of Solidarity of the Latin American Peoples was held in that city July 28-August 5, 1967. One hundred and sixty-four delegates, plus 104 observers and guests, attended the conference, and the usual resolutions were passed. A statement proclaimed, "It is a right and a duty of the peoples of Latin America to carry out the Revolution." "Che" Guevara, at this time embarked on his Bolivian adventure, was "President of Honor" of the conference. He had dispatched a message, published in April in Havana, which had set the theme for the Castro-Communist subversive program: the message called for the creation of "two, three, or many Viet Nams" aimed at completely bogging down the United States in guerrilla wars around the globe.

One would have thought that the conquest of Latin America was a sufficiently ambitious project for Castro and Guevara. Not at all. Their attention to Africa went far beyond inviting African delegates to the Tricontinental Conference. Cuba's designs on the Dark Continent dated back to 1961. Toward the end of that year an office of the Zanzibar National Party was opened in Havana. In mid-1962, at the time when Soviet troops began pouring into Cuba, U.S. intelligence officials were puzzled by reports that a number of Africans had also arrived on the island. As it turned out, they were there to receive indoctrination and training in subversion. Men from at least nine African countries—Ghana, Mali, the Congo, Nigeria, Spanish Guinea, South Africa, Kenya, Tanganyika, and Zanzibar—were given instruction.

Cuba enjoyed the first fruits of its efforts in January 1964. John Okello, an African Negro trained in Cuba, assembled a force of some 600 guerrillas in Zanzibar and led them in successful raids on two police armories. The guerrillas then swept into Zanzibar Town, handed out weapons, and quickly overthrew the pro-Western government. Some of the guerrillas had been trained in Cuba and they sported *fidelista* beards and berets—quite a spectacle in an African capital. The "People's Republic of Zanzibar" was established, and it was promptly recognized by Cuba and the Iron Curtain countries.

"Che" Guevara, the fervent advocate of guerrilla warfare, was the mastermind behind Cuba's vast subversive program. Violence, directed and fueled by Havana, touched virtually every country in Latin America, and in some places it reached dangerous proportions. Nevertheless, the end result that was sought—the establishment of other Communist governments—was not achieved. Guevara's myrmidons approached, but never quite grasped, victory. At some point Guevara decided to relinquish his managerial role, leave Cuba, and go back into the field as a guerrilla commander once again. Guevara had always been a restless individual, and perhaps he had found prolonged residence in one country, Cuba, too confining. Perhaps he had tired of playing second fiddle to Fidel Castro. The continued failures of Cuba's subversive efforts may have convinced him that his personal leadership was required if a guerrilla movement were to succeed.

The disappearance and clandestine travels of Guevara were one of the intelligence feats of the Cold War. Guevara was the top man in Cuba after the Castro brothers, he was a prominent figure in the ranks of international communism, and he was recognized around the world as a guerrilla chieftain and theoretician. For a person of this stature to drop completely out of sight was a unique and bizarre occurrence in modern times. Rumors cropped up that Guevara had appeared in this or that place around the world, but none of these were confirmed, and some experts on Cuban affairs became convinced that Guevara was dead, the victim of either illness or assassination.

Although some of Guevara's travels and activities during the period 1965-1966 remain in mystery, it has now become possible to reconstruct a portion of his wanderings. Evidently disguised as a priest, Guevara secretly slipped out of Cuba and made his way to the Congo, there to lead a guerrilla operation which included a number of Cubans. Guevara had chosen Africa because he believed that, since it was more distant from the United States, a rebel movement there would have a greater chance of success than one in Latin America. In the Congo, at a place called Baraca, Guevara's forces battled troops led by famed mercenary leader Michael Hoare. Years later, in an interview, Hoare described what happened:

> When we arrived at Baraca, which . . . was an amphibious operation, the first thing that impressed itself upon me was the extent of the firepower which was being directed upon us, which was fantastic.
>
> Congolese rebels' tactics would be normally to get drunk on, say, marijuana or something of that nature and to gather in thousands and to come on you in their thousands, overwhelming. But this we didn't experience at Baraca. Here we had troops responding to whistle signals, wearing equipment, carrying out maneuvers, and this went on for four or five days.

Despite the fine combativeness displayed by his men, at least on this occasion, Guevara's African adventure ended disastrously. Details of this fiasco are recounted earlier in this book in the chapter titled "Guevara."

For months afterward the story of Guevara remains a blank. At some point he obtained two Uruguayan passports, made out to false identities. Although these passports were evidently genuine, the information and signatures in one, possibly both, were false, and so it has not been possible to ascertain whether Guevara obtained these in Uruguay, or possibly France (one of the passports may have been sent to the Uruguayan Embassy in Paris), or whether they were obtained by D.G.I. for his use, without his having been in Uruguay or France. At any rate, Guevara eventually returned secretly to Cuba, and there began preparations to launch a guerrilla movement in Bolivia. Guevara's ambitions were still great: his long-range plan was aimed not so much at the Bolivian government as at the entire continent of South America. The Bolivian movement was to serve as a spawning ground for additional guerrilla operations in adjoining countries, and particularly Argentina.

The mounting of the Bolivian movement required extensive intelligence work, in which D.G.I. played a major role. A Bolivian Communist purchased a farm in a hinterland area which was to serve as the guerrillas' base. Guevara, still in disguise, traveled to Spain and Brazil, and slipped into Bolivia early in November 1966. Sixteen Cubans, including high-ranking officers, also traveled to Bolivia, at least one of them passing through the United States. In France, D.G.I. recruited Régis Debray to join and report on Guevara's guerrillas. In Argentina, a man associated with a guerrilla group was summoned to Bolivia, where Guevara gave him detailed instructions on laying the groundwork for a rebel movement in their mutual homeland. For the same purpose, a Communist leader was brought from Peru to confer with Guevara. A D.G.I. official who used the code name "Ivan" served as a liaison between Guevara and Havana. Another D.G.I. official, René Martínez Tamayo (code name: "Arturo"), was Guevara's radio and explosives expert and died with him in Bolivia.

For, despite all the planning and preparations, Guevara's hopes came to naught. After eleven months of ambushes and skirmishes, Guevara was captured and executed by the Bolivian army. The Bolivian adventure had been far more successful as an intelligence operation than as a guerrilla rebellion. For D.G.I. it had been a project carried out on an international scale, and D.G.I.'s role in the affair did not terminate with "Che's" death. (See "Guevara" chapter.)

That D.G.I. was able to carry out its tasks on so wide a scale was an indication of how large and effective Fidel Castro's espionage service had grown since "Section M" of the Department of State Security became the nucleus of a new intelligence organization. Following are details on the structure and personnel of D.G.I.

The headquarters in Havana is known as the *Centro Principal.* The major staffs are called "sections," and these in turn are divided into desks. The Principal Center is divided into ten sections, five of which handle operations, while the other five are of a support nature. The operational sections, and their areas of responsibility, are:

Section II-1	Latin America
Section II-2	Western Europe
Section III	Offices in Moscow, Prague, East Germany, Canada, Mexico, the United Nations
Section III-1	Illegals
Section V	Africa and Middle East

The support sections are:

Section III-2	Contacts

Section IV	Personnel
Section M-1	Technical services
Documentation Center	
Logistics	

The work and personnel of the ten sections are as follows:

Sections II-1 and II-2. The overall chief is "Armando." He was the official at the Principal Center who was in charge of D.G.I. activities related to Guevara's Bolivian operation.

Section II-1. "Ariel" is chief of this section under "Armando." "Ariel" is responsible for the six branches into which Latin America is divided. The six branches, and their branch chiefs, are:

Colombia / Venezuela / Ecuador	"Arana"
Brazil / Uruguay	"Fermin"
Argentina / Chile / Peru	"José Luis"
Dominican Republic / Haiti / Jamaica	"Jesus"
Guatemala / Central America	"Noel"
Bolivia	"Lino

Chiefs of country desks within the Section II-1 branches include "Gary," chief of the Uruguayan desk, and "Jordan," chief of the Peruvian desk. "Gary" uses as his cover a position with the Cuban Institute of Friendship with Peoples (I.C.A.P.). Among the personnel attached to Section II-1 is "Renan," who as "Ivan" served as a liaison between D.G.I. and Guevara in Bolivia. "Renan" bears a strong resemblance to movie actor Kirk Douglas.

Section II-1 maintains centers only in those hemisphere countries with which Cuba has diplomatic relations: Mexico, Jamaica, and Chile. Some of Section II-1's activities are handled through the Intelligence Center in Paris. The Paris Center takes care of agents traveling through that city en route to or from Havana, and it establishes letter drops used by revolutionaries under the jurisdiction of II-1, forwarding their correspondence to Havana.

On occasion, Section II-1 officers travel abroad. In October 1967 the chief of the Dominican branch, "Jesus," traveled to Paris to meet the Dominican leader, Francisco Alberto Caamaño. In November 1968 "Noel," the chief of the Guatemala/Central America Branch, went to Paris to meet Ricardo Ramírez de Leon, a leader of a Guatemalan revolutionary organization.

Section II-2. "Julio" is the chief of this section. He personally supervises French, Austrian, Swiss, Portuguese, and possibly Spanish matters. His deputy is "José." Section II-2 has seven country desks, each with five to eight officials. The desks: Austria, France/Belgium,

Italy, Portugal, Spain, Switzerland, and the United Kingdom. Each desk is responsible for supporting its respective overseas center. Chief of the Italian desk is either "David," former head of the D.G.I. center in Rome, or Roberto Alvarez Barrera ("Remigio"). Alvarez was formerly assigned to Paris, where his cover position was that of Second Secretary of the Cuban Mission to U.N.E.S.C.O. In 1968 he was in charge of organizing participation of French youths in summer work and indoctrination camps in Cuba. "Orestes" is chief of the Spanish desk. He was formerly First Secretary of the Cuban Embassy in Madrid. Chief of the French/Belgian desk is "Janio." Among the personnel in Section II-2 are: "Leyda," wife of section chief "Julio" and a member of the Cuban delegation to the General Assembly of U.N.E.S.C.O., a specialist in diplomatic affairs and business management procedures; "Magaly," who is responsible for counter-intelligence and for contacts with journalists; "Manolo," who was trained in the Soviet Union; "Taimara," also trained in the Soviet Union; and "Isnoel," responsible for scientific and technical matters.

The overseas centers of Section II-2 are located within the Cuban diplomatic posts in Geneva, Lisbon, London, Madrid, Paris, Rome, and Vienna. The *Centro* in Vienna is the newest, having been opened in the spring of 1968. There are no centers in Scandinavia, although it is believed D.G.I. plans to open one in Stockholm. Cuba closed its diplomatic mission in Athens in 1968, and Cuban interest in Greece are handled by the Cuban Embassy in Rome. Presumably any intelligence matters related to Greece are managed by the D.G.I. center in Rome. In Belgium, D.G.I. affairs were handled by a collaborator, Luis Palacios Rodríguez, who was Second Secretary of the Cuban Embassy in Brussels. In The Hague, D.G.I. was represented by Aldo Rodríguez Camps ("Aldo"), who was the Commercial Counselor of the Cuban Mission.

Among the D.G.I. personnel in Europe are/were the following:

Center	Names and other data	Position
Geneva	Santiago Díaz Pas ("Rodrigo"). Has cover position with U.N. office in Geneva.	Chief
Lisbon	Mario García Vázquez ("Daniel").	Chief
London	Cristobal Fajardo Rabassa ("Abel").	Chief
Madrid	Aristides Díaz Rovirosa ("Domingo").	Chief
	Orlando Kautzman Torres	Official
	His wife may also work for D.G.I.	

102

Paris	Armando López Orta ("Arquimides"). Was recalled as result of Orlando Castro's defection.	Chief
Rome	Adalberto Marrero Rodríguez. Was formerly Chief of Logistics at Principal Center. Wife is also believed to be D.G.I. official.	Chief
	"Oneido." Trained in Soviet Union.	Official
Vienna	"Armando." Trained in Soviet Union.	Chief

Section III. This section is divided into nine subsections: Central Intelligence Agency (C.I.A.), Counter-Revolution, United Nations, Mexico, Canada, Soviet Union, Czechoslovakia, East Germany, and a false documents unit. Head of Section III is "Demetrio," who came to D.G.I. from the Department of State Security (D.S.E.) in August 1966. In D.S.E. he had been chief of "Section L," which was charged with surveillance of foreign diplomatic missions in Havana.

In the mid-sixties an office of Section III called the C.I.A. and Counter-Revolution Bureau had as its objective to penetrate C.I.A. and Cuban exile activities directed against the Castro regime. In August 1966 "Jacobo" was placed in charge of the C.I.A. group. He was a former officer of D.S.E.'s "Section L." "Candido," also a former D.S.E. officer, was put in charge of the Counter-Revolution unit. In 1967 the Bureau was split, and the men remained as chiefs of the now separate desks.

The United Nations desk supports the activities of the D.G.I. *Centro* within the Cuban Mission to the United Nations. Most of the mission officials work for D.G.I. The U.N. Center maintains contact with subversive organizations in the United States, serves as a funnel for Cuban propaganda to enter this country, and through its agents, particularly in the Miami area, keeps track of the activities of Cuban exile organizations. It is Castro's espionage outpost within the United States.

The unit responsible for false documents is called "Diosdado's Group." The formal name of the unit is not known. This is the name by which it is always called, because it is headed by an official who uses the code name "Diosdado." It acquires the seals, stamps, and stationery of foreign embassies, as well as different types of paper from foreign countries. It secures maps, train schedules, photographs of airports, information about frontiers, and in general all types of information that may be useful to D.G.I. officials traveling abroad, including details on how foreign borders may be crossed illegally.

The D.G.I. center in Mexico City is responsible for supporting clandestine operations in that country as well as in the rest of Latin America, particularly Central America. Since Mexico City is one of the few places which still maintains a regular air route with Havana, the Mexico *Centro* assists the comings and goings of agents and subversive figures. The *Centro* also arranges for agents to be slipped across the border into the United States. Because of the variety of tasks carried out by this key office, its staff members probably are under the jurisdiction of more than one of the D.G.I. sections, although basically it functions as a part of Section III.

D.G.I. officials now or recently assigned to Mexico City include the following:

Name	*Cover position at Embassy, Consulate*
Felix Luna Mederos	First Secretary
("Filiberto"), chief of Centro	
Rafael Mirabel Fernández	Vice Consul, Attache
Edgardo Obulio	Commercial Attache
Valdés Suarez	
Enrique Micuel Cicard	Consul General,
Labrada	Third Secretary
Lineo Fernando	Consul
Salazar Chia	
Juan Astorga	Employee
Frometa	
Luis Ismael Cruz Arce	Consul
Jesus Cruz González	Second Secretary

The Section III center in Prague arranges for the travel, housing, and documentation of leftist revolutionaries en route to Cuba for training or consultation. Antonio Perez Caneiro ("Nico") is the chief of the center. His cover position is that of First Secretary of the Cuban Embassy. His brother, Ricardo Perez Caneiro, is also a D.G.I. official and also holds the position of First Secretary.

The centers in the Soviet Union and East Germany serve as liaisons with the intelligence services of those countries. The Moscow *Centro* handles Cuban personnel sent to that country for intelligence training.

The D.G.I. center in Canada serves as an outlet for propaganda, handles agents slipping into or out of the United States, and is in touch with subversive separatist movements. For months in 1963 the city of Quebec was troubled by terrorists who were setting fires and placing bombs in public buildings. After intensive investigations, the police arrested seventeen members of an organization called *Front de Libération Québecois.* Among the leaders who were jailed was a former University of Montreal student, Georges Schoeters, who had met Castro during a trip the latter made to Montreal. Subsequently, Schoeters took two trips to Cuba, one of them of several months' duration, during which time he is believed to have been given instruction in subversive techniques.

Section III-1. Sometime between mid-1967 and early 1968 Section III (Illegals) was divided into two separate entities: Section III and Section III-1, which became the "illegal" section. Section III retained most of the operational units of the former section, as described above. Section III-1 is engaged in such activities as recruitment, training, and infiltration. It is headed by "Lucio." A subsection, referred to by the code name of its chief, "Dario," is believed to have some responsibility for activities in other Communist countries.

Section III-2. This section, called *Enlaces,* provides D.G.I. officials abroad with mail drops, safe houses, meeting sites, and accommodation addresses. It also handles liaison with other organizations of the Cuban government, including D.S.E. "Quero" is the chief of the section. His deputy is Adalberto Quintana Suarez ("Sexto"),* who is also Vice-Director of the Cuban Institute of Friendship with Peoples. Section III-2 maintains a file on clandestine contact facilities throughout the world, available for any D.G.I. operation.

Section IV. Called *Cuadros,* this section is responsible for the recruitment and training of all D.G.I. staff personnel. It also selects personnel for the diplomatic courier service. The chief is believed to be "Pelayo." Another high official is Ramiro Rodríguez Gomez, who was the chief of the D.G.I. *Centro* in Rio de Janeiro from 1961 until Brazil severed relations with Cuba in 1964.

Section M-1. This section supplies clandestine communications systems to D.G.I. personnel, as well as any technical support that may be needed. The section's facilities include an audio unit, a

---

*Quintana was at one time *Centro* chief in Paris. Among his clandestine contacts was a French woman named Michèle Firk. Firk committed suicide in September 1968 in Guatemala City in order to avoid arrest by Guatemalan authorities for her alleged participation in the assassination of U.S. Ambassador John Mein.

105

photographic unit, a concealment devices unit, and a codes and secret-writing unit.

Documentation Center. This office takes care of official documents used by D.G.I. personnel in their travels. The chief is "Facundo."

Logistics Section. This section handles the food, clothing, and housing needs of officials coming to Havana, as well as the logistic and administrative needs of the various departments in the Principal Center.

Cuba's interest in Africa and increasing interest in the Middle East has augmented the importance of Section V, which is responsible for both areas. Armando Ulises Estrada Fernández ("Ulises") is the chief of Section V. He works closely with his military counterpart, Major Victor Emiliano Dreke Cruz, an official of the Ministry of the Revolutionary Armed Forces, of which Raúl Castro is chief. Dreke is in charge of Cuban army operations in Africa (there are Cuban military units stationed at Brazzaville), as well as of Cuban guerrilla activities in that continent.

Estrada traveled to the Middle East in early 1969 and visited camps of the Al Fatah Arab guerrilla organization. He accompanied Arab raiders on an incursion into Israeli-occupied territory.

The *escuelas especiales* (special schools) which had been run by D.G.I. for the guerrilla training of foreign nationals was transferred to the Armed Forces Ministry in February 1967. D.G.I. and the ministry coordinate in this enterprise, and it is believed that Estrada may head a school which has given training to members of Al Fatah. Abu al-Hasan, an official of Al Fatah, stated in April 1970: "Some time ago a group of our combatants was graduated from the Havana military college. We were the first Asian group admitted to this college. At the graduation the college commandant, who happened to have spent some time with us in the Jordan Valley, said: 'I present to you today a class of legendary guerrilla fighters from Asia—Al Asifah fighters.' " (Al-Asifah is the military wing of Al Fatah.)

The geographical extensiveness of D.G.I.'s operations attests to the importance attached to its work by the Castro government. D.G.I. is an expanding organization. In addition to its own structure, it has virtually taken over the Prensa Latina news agency and the Cuban Institute for Friendship with Peoples (I.C.A.P.). The latter is in charge of the many foreigners who visit Cuba for one reason or another. D.G.I. officials have moved into Cuba's diplomatic corps to such an extent that this has become hardly more than an arm of the intelligence service. In Africa and the Middle East, where Cuba's

106

diplomatic aims and intelligence designs are one and the same, most Cuban ambassadors are D.G.I. and double as chiefs of *centros*.

The United States itself has not been beyond the reach of Castro's intelligence organization. It has, in fact, long been an area of primary interest. When Castro was still a guerrilla in the Sierra Maestra mountains, his agents in the States carried out propaganda activities and arranged for the shipment of weapons to the rebels. Following Castro's rise to power, his agents have continued highly active in this country.

In 1959 two of his agents attempted to bribe two Florida police officers and an F.B.I. agent pretending to be a local officer to arrange the kidnapping of a man wanted by the Cuban government. In a reverse operation, two American flyers in a small plane were shot down over Cuba in March 1960 as they participated in a scheme to make it appear that the United States was involved in helping "war criminals" escape from Cuba. (Their being shot down was apparently due to an accident.) The Americans had been bribed by a Castro agent in the States.

This same agent—a naturalized American citizen—kept Havana informed of the activities of Cuban exiles in Florida and was believed responsible for the capture in Cuba of a number of exiles who participated in clandestine missions to that country. This agent circulated freely in the exile community, and was particularly well-informed about missions to Cuba because of his work on small boats in the Miami area. To trasmit information to Havana, he sent coded messages by telephone and commercial cable, and he was also in contact with the Cuban Intelligence Center at the United Nations. This agent still lives in Miami; because his activities have not directly involved espionage against the United States, charges have not been brought against him.

Cuba has never had any real difficulty in infiltrating agents into the United States. When one considers that more than 900 Cuban refugees enter the country every week, it is understandable that D.G.I. is able to get personnel into this country. Most of the refugees arrive via the daily Varadero-Miami airlift; others come in small boats. Still others are flown in from the Guantánamo Naval Base, having jumped over the fence there and asked for asylum. And still more eventually make their way to the States after having flown from Havana to Spain or Mexico. Refugees are screened by U.S. officials, but there is no sure way of weeding out all the men and women who may be working for D.G.I.

In the fall of 1965, when Castro permitted flotillas of small boats to leave Cuba filled with refugees heading for the States, a D.G.I. official began recruiting large numbers of the refugees to work for the Intelligence service once they arrived north. Rather than endanger their hopes of leaving, the refugees agreed to the official's demands. Some of them evidently took seriously their promise to help: D.G.I. began receiving reports from a number of them. The official had failed, however, to instruct his recruits on how to identify themselves when sending their reports, and when these began arriving, D.G.I. was unable to determine who was sending them. The reports were virtually useless.

Groups of leftist American students have visited Cuba over the years. Radical black leaders, such as Stokely Carmichael and Robert Williams, have also been in Cuba. The Castro government encourages subversive movements in the States by radio broadcasts, by playing host to these visitors, and probably by giving some of them basic training in subversive techniques.

Among pro-Castro "front" groups established in the United States have been the Medical Aid for Cuba Committee and the Fair Play for Cuba Committee. The latter organization was spotlighted when a person associated with it, Lee Harvey Oswald, assassinated President John F. Kennedy in November 1963. Although there has been no indication that Castro had any hand in the assassination, it is not inconceivable that he had an inkling it might be attempted. Oswald was in Mexico from September 26 until October 3 of 1963, and during that time he visited the Cuban Embassy in Mexico City, ostensibly seeking a visa to enter Cuba. A few weeks earlier, Castro had warned that if American leaders were involved in plans against his regime, "they themselves will not be safe."

Because the United States and Cuba do not maintain diplomatic relations, and therefore there is no Cuban diplomatic mission accredited to this country, the Intelligence *Centro* at the United Nations serves as headquarters for Cuban-directed subversive and espionage activities in the States. There have been a number of cases in which the United States has had to take action against Cuban United Nations officials because of their intelligence activities.

In November 1962, the F.B.I. arrested three Cubans in New York and seized a cache of explosives and incendiary devices. The Cubans were charged with attempting to gather information about U.S. military installations and with stockpiling the explosives "for the purpose of injuring and destroying national defense materials, premises, and utilities." Among the contemplated targets were retail stores, oil refineries, and the New York subway system. The detainees included Roberto Santiestebán Casanova, an attaché at the Cuban Mission. Because he had arrived recently, his official papers were being processed and the U.S. government asserted he still did not enjoy diplomatic immunity. A Cuban couple, José Gómez Abad and his wife Elisa Montero de Gómez Abad, were charged with complicity in the affair and ordered to leave the country. Both were attachés at the Mission, and as such did have diplomatic immunity from arrest.

In January 1968 Chafik Homero Saker Zenni (who also used the name Rolo Martínez; code name "Rolo"), First Secretary of the Cuban Mission, was barred from reentering the United States. In February 1969 Jesus Jimenez Escobar, Counselor of the Mission, was also refused reentry. Both men had been providing guidance and financial assistance to black extremist groups in the States.

In August 1969, Lázaro Eddy Espinosa Bonet, Third Secretary of the Mission, was ordered expelled because he had attempted to recruit several Cuban refugees for the purpose—the United States said succinctly—of gathering information about "the security of the office of the President." The fact was that, meeting clandestinely with Espinosa in New York, the refugees had been instructed to obtain all the information they could about President Nixon's home on Key Biscayne in Miami: photographs, floor plans, details of security, itineraries, and modes of travel used by the president when arriving and leaving. It is not known why D.G.I. wanted this information.

At the same time that Espinosa was expelled, the United States also barred Alberto Boza-Hidalgo Gato (code name "Zabo"), who was in Cuba at the time, from reentering the country. Boza-Hidalgo, First Secretary of the Cuban U.N. Mission, was charged with attempting to recruit refugees for the purpose of gathering "material of an intelligence value" about a U.S. military installation.

In October 1970 another espionage case involving Cuba's U.N. Mission was revealed. Orlando Gutiérrez, First Secretary of the Mission, and Rogelio Rodríguez Lopez ("José"), Counselor of the Mission, were given forty-eight hours to leave the United States by the U.S. government. They had been using the services of a young secretary employed at the Washington embassy of the Republic of South Africa. The secretary's access to embassies and cocktail parties had been useful to the Cubans, whose diplomatic activities are officially limited to the New York area.

These are cases that have been partially brought to view. Other operations continue in the gray world of espionage. D.G.I., in the

United States as well as elsewhere in the world, relentlessly pursues its goal of attempting to subvert other nations to the Communist standard. As D.G.I. grows larger, its operations become more sophisticated, its tentacles extend farther and farther abroad, and it steadily becomes a more deadly instrument.

SECRETO DE ESTADO

La Habana, junio 23 de 1967
"AÑO DEL VIET NAM HEROICO"

Dr Baudilio Castellanos
Embajador de Cuba
París.
Francia.

Estimado Baudilio :

Recibí tu carta en la que nos informas sobre la proposición de venta de buques de guerra hecha por un francés.

En la misma planteas que ya has pedido datos al Ministerio de Defensa de dicho país.

Si hubieras avisado antes, te hubieramos orientado que en vez de visitar dicho Ministerio, fueras al de Rela--ciones Exteriores y por las vias usuales, explicar la - proposición que te hicieron, pero que tu, antes de en--viar el informe de esto a Cuba, quieres consultar con - dicho Ministerio, porque tienes instrucciones de nues--tro Gobierno, de que no debemos hacer nada que pueda --perjudicar al Gobierno Francés, por lo tanto, antes de informarnos a nosotros, deseas saber la opinión de ellos sobre esa institución o individuo que te hizo la propo-sición, y sí en caso de que Cuba aceptara comprar los - barcos, qué decisión tomaría el Gobierno Francés. Esto debes hacerlo como una gestión personal tuya.

No tenemos interés en adquirir dichas armas, pero consideramos de gran importancia, tantear la actitud del Go-bierno Francés sobre la posibilidad de que decidan ven-dernos algún armamento si asi lo solicitáramos.

Creo que es suficiente para que comprendas la idea. No sabemos si la respuesta del Ministerio de Defensa, deja sin lugar la consulta al Min Rex de allí, de todas maneras, debes actuar como estimes pertinente, dentro del --

Letter from Raúl Castro to Ambassador Castellanos regarding possibility of buying French weapons.

marco de estas instrucciones, sabiendo ya el punto que —
nos interesa.

Transmite mi saludo a tu esposa e hijos,

Abrazos de,

Cmdte Raúl Castro Ruz.

:fp

Reg Salida #00120

Relaciones entre los Jefes de Centros y los Jefes de las Misiones
diplomáticas punto aparte

1-) Es necesario poner en conocimiento del Jefe de la Misión coma
siempre con previa entre el Departamento(Comandante Piñeiro) y el
Ministerio de Relaciones Exteriores(Dr. Roa) la existencia de un
Centro en las Embajadas o Misiones Cubanas en el extranjero punto
aparte

Al Jefe de la Misión se le comunica oficialmente que las tareas de
los Centros serán las de obtener Informaciones Secretas y Super-
Secreta de interés especial para la República Cubana punto aparte
En cada caso especifico coma al Jefe de la Misión se le pone en conocimiento coma en forma correspondiente coma de que entre los debe-
res de los Centros esta el de garantizar la Seguridad de la Embajada
y su personal coma así como de los secretos de Estado punto. En el
cumplimiento de estas tareas deben interesarse en grado igual coma
el Jefe y Jefe de la Misión punto aparte.

2) El Jefe del Centro es presentado al Jefe de la Misión en el
Territorio Cubano o en la Embajada República Cubana coma según las
circunstancias punto aparte.

3- La distribución de las obligaciones y tareas del personal diplo-
mático y técnico de la Embajada coma debe realizarse mediante recí-
proca colaboración entre Jefe de la Misión y el Jefe del Centro(de
esta manera el Jefe del Centro tendrá posibilidad de dar a los oficiales el trabajo que le permita desarrollar sus tareas especial de
Inteligencia punto aparte.

4) El Oficial de Inteligencia que trabaja en el extranjero tiene
que cumplir sus obligaciones diplomáticas y administrativas coma
para así merecer las consideraciones y ayuda del Jefe de la Misión
punto EN CAso de que el Jefe del Centro tenga necesidad de salir del
Edificio de la Embajada durante las horas de trabajo coma debera
comunicarlo al Jefe de la Misión coma indicandole la hora de em-
pezar regreso punto Los demás oficiales del Centro usaran pretextos
" oficiales" para su salida de la Embajada coma tal como dos puntos
de visitar al médico coma necesidad de realizar funciones propias
de su cargo en la Embajada coma para hacer compras como ayuda a su
familia coma etcétera punto.

5) El Jefe de la Misión debe tener conocimiento oficial de que el
Jefe del Centro tiene derecho a utilizar los medios de comunicación
dada por valijas diplomáticas coma así como las cifradas punto aparte

Instructions regarding relations between D.G.I. *centro* chiefs and heads
of Cuban diplomatic missions.

AST: <u>COMUNICACIONES AL CP.</u>

En el futuro, toda comunicación a este CP, en la que se traten asuntos relativos a ciudadanos latinoamericanos, deberá venir dirigida a JULIO/ARANA si se trata de venezolanos, JULIO/JOSE LUIS si se trata de argentinos, y - así sucesivamente. Al final del presente aparecen los nombres de los compañeros de II-1 y los países que los mismos atienden.

Esto se refiere fundamentalmente a los cables que ustedes nos envían. Viniendo de la forma señalada anteriormente, garantizamos una mayor agilidad en la recepción de la copia del cable por parte del compañero que atiende el país de que se trate.

Si dichos cables requieren respuesta, la misma será - - coordinada previamente aquí, según consideración que al efecto se ha llevado a cabo con el compañero ARLEL.

Esta modalidad en el envío de cables incluye aquellos - en que se nos anuncia recepción de correspondencia, telegramas, etc., de los buzones existentes en Francia. - Según el país del remitente, así deberán ustedes remitirnos el cable. Es decir, si el B-20 recibió corres-- pondencia de Venezuela, el cable del CP debe venir dirigido JULIO/ARANA.

Se exceptúan de esta disposición los cables y comunicaciones relativas a latinoamericanos que sean casos del- Centro y cuya atención y dirección correspondan exclusivamente a II.-2.

Instructions from *Centro Principal* in Havana to Paris *centro* regarding messages dealing with Latin Americans.

AT: JULIO
AS: SOBRE (1). *CURA* .. (2)... *MUGICA* ....

ESTE (1). *CURA* .... DE NACIONALIDAD (3). *Argentino* ....
SE PRESENTO EN ESTA POR EL MES DE NOVIEMBRE DEL AÑO PASADO
PRESENTANDOME UNA CONTRASEÑA QUE YO HABIA ACORDADO CON (4) *Ali-*
cia. appele ...ASI QUE CON UNA CARTA DE LA MISMA. EL OBJETIVO
ERA VIAJAR A CUBA. COMO ES COSTUMBRE EN ESTOS CASOS COMUNICAMOS
EL ASUNTO A ARIEL Y ESTE NOS DIO LA AUTORIZACION PARA QUE (2)..
.S... *MUGICA*. VIAJARA.
(2)..... *MUGICA* .... NOS PLANTEO QUE EL PENSABA QUE-
DARSE AQUI UNOS MESES ESTUDIANDO, LEYENDO. QUE PENSABA VIAJAR
POR EL MES DE FEBRERO.
DESPUES DE ESTA SU PRIMERA VISITA LO INVITE A COMER PARA CHARLAR
UN RATO. EN ESA OCASION LE PEDI ME ENTREGARA UNA RELACION DE LOS
(5). *Latino Americanos* ... QUE EL CONOCIERA. ESTA
PETICION SE LA HICE SIN PRECISARLE DETALLES, UN INTERES PRECISO,
ERA LA SEGUNDA O TERCERA VEZ QUE LO VEIA.
DESPUES DE ESA REUNION DEJE CAER LAS RELACIONES AL NIVEL DE
ORIGEN, NO LE PLANTEE MAS NADA, LO RECIBIA EN LA OFICINA, CON-
VERSABAMOS DE DIFERENTES TOPICOS YA QUE TUVE EL TEMOR DE EMBAR-
CARME EN UN TRABAJO QUE POR LAS CARACTERISTICAS QUE VEIA EN EL
EN ESOS MOMENTOS PODIA SER PELIGROSO, PODRIA RESULTAR UN DESAS-
TRE.
SU ACTIVIDAD AQUI, LAS QUE EL PENSABA REALIZAR Y REALIZO, RESUL-
TABA QUEMANTE, PARTICIPABA EN REUNIONES PARA ESTUDIAR TAL O MAS
CUAL TEMA, ES DECIR, REFLECCIONAR, COMO EL DICE, SOBRE LA
PROBLEMATICA DE LA REVOLUCION Y LA (6). *Iglesia.*, PARTICI-
PABA EN CONFERENCIAS DONDE ERA EL EL CONFERENCISTA Y EN ALGUNOS
CASOS SE CONOCIA SU VINCULACION CON NOSOTROS, CONMIGO, ME PRESEN-
TABA INDIVIDUOS, (1). *CURAS*. COMO EL, A LOS CUALES HABIA
CONOCIDO AQUI Y POR HABER REFLECCIONADO UN POCO YA EL TIPO LE
PARECIA FORMIDABLE. ESTA ACTITUD INDISCRETA SE MANIFESTO AL
ENCONTRARSE UNA VEZ CON DANIEL EN UNA EXPOSICION Y LE DIJO, SEGUN
DANIEL (ESTO LO SEÑALE EN UN INFORME SOBRE DANIEL) QUE YO LE

Message regarding Argentine priest who wanted to go to Cuba and who
gave the proper countersign.

152/CF

AT   : JULIO

AST : ENVIO DE UN ESCONDRIJO.

ANX : (4) CUATRO CROQUIS CON SUS LEYENDAS.

(3) FOTOS CON SUS DESCRIPCIONES.

-IDENTIFICACION DEL ESCONDRIJO : ERNESTICO 4/69.

-NOMBRE DEL ESCONDRIJO........ : TABAC BOUQUET D'AUTEUIL,

-DIRECCION DEL LUGAR.......... : 8, RUE D'AUTEUIL Y PLACE
D'AUTEUIL, PARIS 16.

-DESPUES DE HABER HECHO UNA OFENSIVA EN LO QUE RESPECTA A LOS "LUGARES DE CONTACTOS"; DAMOS COMIENZO A OTRA NUEVA OFENSIVA, - PERO ESTA VEZ SERA A LOS "ESCONDRIJOS" Y EN UNA FORMA MUY VARIADA,- COMO TAMBIEN SE TRABAJARA SOBRE LA OBTENCION DE OTROS RECURSOS OPERA TIVOS Y SOBRE AQUELLOS QUE MAS NECESITE EL C. P.

1- CON LA CONFECCION DE ESTE ESCONDRIJO, PODEMOS OBSERVAR EL CRITERIO DE TRABAJO QUE HA OBTENIDO "ERNESTICO", EL CUAL YA SE - DESENVUELVE MUY BIEN EN LA CONFECCION Y ESTUDIOS DE ESTOS RECURSOS- OPERATIVOS. -ESPERAMOS QUE LOS CRITERIOS DE TRABAJO DE ERNESTICO SE AMPLIEN Y MAS AHORA QUE IRA DE VACACIONES PARA ESA.

SALUDOS REVOLUCIONARIOS :

OSVALDO.

On carrying out a "new offensive" –the finding of potential hiding places.

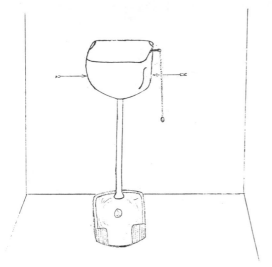

A potential hiding place
for messages.

Message regarding house
where person can hide.

IVES PARIS, lo conozco desde hace 4 años.

Dirección de la casa que sirve para: 1 - contacto

　　　　　　　　　　　　　　　　　　 2 - alojamiento por una semana
　　　　　　　　　　　　　　　　　　　　 máximo.

9, rue Victor Cousin

PARIS V

Tiene una casa de campo "LES MARGOTTONS"

　　　　　　　　　 par ARTHON

　　　　　　　　　　 INDRE

a 260 Km. de París.

Ver plan adjunto. Allí se puede alojar una persona todo el tiempo
que sea, avisando con tiempo a IVES. Es una casa vieja donde se
puede pasar completamente desapercibido. Hay dos casas vecinas:
una de un campesino que está acostumbrado a ver llegar gente y
otra de dos viejecitas de 80 años.

IVES sería responsable de una red de tres buzones, gente amiga de
él y de absoluta confianza.

AST: CUESTIONES RELACIONADAS CON (1) *Congo Brazaville*

Los compañeros de V han sabido que (2) *Agboli Jean Joalee*
(3).. *Frances*.. y vicepresidente de la (4). *Federación*...
de (6). *Estudiantes*..... del (7).. *Africa Negra*.........en
(3).... *Francia*... y (8). *Martin Bemba*..., (9). *Congoles*
........, presidente de la Asociación de (6). *Estudiantes*
(9).. *Congoleses*.... en (3).. *Francia*.... , están en el —
(1).. *Congo-B.*.... con el objetivo de discutir con los –
dirigentes (9).. *Congoceses*... sobre el caso (10). *Mulele*.
...... la situación política del país y el caso del (11)
.... *MNL*... de (12). *Camerun*...... A este (11).. *MNL*.. no
se le permiten actividades en el territorio (9). *Congoles*
debido a errores cometidos por los dirigentes del mismo y
a la situación del (1).. *Congo-B*.... con los demás   paí—
ses limítrofes.

Se ha podidio conocer que los (6).. *Estudiantes*.. de dichas
organizaciones tienen opinión contraria al regimen del —
(1)... *Congo-B*..........

(2). *Agboli Jean Joalle*....... le informóa nuestro (13). *Embajador*.......
que también se reunirían con las (14).. *Embajadas*.... (15)
.. *Socialistas*.... acreditadas en (1).. *Congo-B*...

Ademá s le dijo que en el Congreso último que celebraron-
los (6).. *Estudiantes*..... (9). *congoleses*.. en (3) *Francia*..
se plantearon las cuestiones que ellos van a discutir con
los dirigentes (9). *congoleses*. y que el Congreso estuvo en
cendido.

Por otro lado se supo que un (9). *congoles*.. de (16).....
.. *Kinshasa*..... llamado (17). *Yerodia*. está detrás de
toda esta agitación en el caso (10). *Mulele*... y en la –
posición contraria al (1). *Congo-B*.. A este individuo—

lo habían nombrado en (1)..*Congés..*..., director de la
radio y no aceptó. Se quedó en (5).*París*...

Los compañeros de V necesitan saber si mediante algún ––
vínculo en el círculo o en las organizaciones menciona––
das se podría conocer:

1.– Si es cierto que dichos individuos tienen los car––
gos que se señalan, sus posiciones políticas y todo cuan
to sobre ellos se pueda obtener.

2.– Sobre el Congreso último que tuvieron los (09).....
Congoleses, en (3).*Francia*.. y si en el mismo se mane-
jaron esos elementos y quién los llevó al mismo.

3.– Qué posición mantiene (17)..*Verodia*...., qué hace,
qué tipo de actividad ha desarrollado en relación con el
caso (10).*Malele*.. y qué objetivos puede perseguir.

Deberá informarse por cable cualquier dato concreto que-
se pueda conocer sobre lo anterior.

                    – = o O o = –

Message about activities of two student leaders in the Congo.

AST: SOBRE PLAN ROMANO

De acuerdo a las conversaciones que tuvimos en ésta con GARY
sobre el Plan Especial que debía desarrollarse en ésa, sólo-
queda concretar las cuestiones que están en manos de ustedes.
En lo que respecta a la parte de los compañeros de II-1 es--
tán listos para llevar a vías de hecho la Operación.

A modo de recordarte las cuestiones que ustedes deben llevar-
a cabo en ésa, pasamos a enumerártelas:

1.- Selección de la persona que llevaría el material y eje-
cutaría la Operación.

2.- Estudio y selección de la casa adecuada para realizar -
el trabajo, pudiendo nosotros informarte que de acuerdo a --
las prácticas ya realizadas en esta, solamente necesitaría--
mos tres días como máximo para realizar el trabajo.

3.- Conocimiento de los requisitos aduanales para sacar el
material de Europa tales como: tiempo que debe permanecer -
rodando el auto en el país antes de poder sacarlo, papeles -
necesarios para viajar con el mismo, si antes de embarcarlo-
lo pesan, costo del mismo siendo del año 1961, qué inspección
le hacen en el puerto, si se necesita una licencia de conduc
ción internacional.

Todos estos aspectos serían necesarios, lógicamente, pues --
complementarían la información que actualmente poseemos. En
fin, por parte nuestra estamos listos para comenzar a traba-
jar en la operación. Esta se llamará en lo adelante PLAN RO
MANO.

- = o O o = -

Instructions regarding "Plan Romano" – smuggling arms concealed in
cars into Venezuela.